The Door I Shut Behind Me
Selected Fiction, Poetry and Drama

Uma Parameswaran

AFFILIATED EAST-WEST PRESS (P) LTD.
New Delhi Madras Bangalore Hyderabad

AFFILIATED EAST-WEST PRESS PVT. LTD.

G-1/16, Ansari Road, New Delhi-110 002
1/1, General Patters Road, Madras 600 002
35-36, Greames Road, Madras-600 006
100, Bima Nagar (LIC Colony), Hyderabad-500 380
5, Lavelle Road, Sixth Cross, Bangalore 560 001

© 1990 Uma Parameswaran

Price: Rs. 40.00

ISBN: 81 85336 35 0

Some of these poems first appeared in the following journals:
Canadian Ethnic Studies, Chandrabhaga, Commonwealth Quarterly, Fame '86, Journal of Indian Writing in English, Journal of South Asian Literature, Toronto South Asian Review, Writers Workshop.

Trishanku and *Rootless but Green are the Boulevard Trees* first published in Canada in 1988 by TSAR Publications.

Cover art by Lalitha Thyagarajan
Printed at T.T. Maps & Publications Limited,
328, G.S.T. Road, Chromepet, Madras 600 044.
Published by Affiliated East-West Press Pvt. Ltd.,
25, Dr. Muniappa Road, Kilpauk, Madras 600 010.

Contents

	Page
Introduction	v
The Door I Shut Behind Me	1
Trishanku	17
Rootless but Green are the Boulevard Trees	95

Introduction

I have known Uma Parameswaran for many years as a professor at the University of Winnipeg. Only more recently have I become familiar with her writing, which is distinguished by many of the same characteristics which make Dr. Parameswaran so delightful a colleague and friend: curiosity about people and insight into their ways, a wise tolerance of human foibles, intelligence and humour. When editing an anthology of South Asian Canadian Literature for Toronto South Asian Review, I had occasion to study her works more closely, and found her treatment of the theme of Indo-Canadian experience in different genres particularly intriguing. The appearance of this volume, which brings together three works—a sequence of poems, a short story, and a play—interconnected by theme and by recurring characters, is therefore very welcome.

Uma Parameswaran's writing career spans a number of years. Her early work appeared in newspapers in India, and she received her M.A. in Creative Writing from Indiana University, with a thesis consisting of four short stories. *The Door I Shut Behind Me*, whose protagonist Chander would reappear in her later work, won the 1967 Lady Eaton Award. Following her move to Winnipeg in 1966, she has been very active in writing plays and scripts for the local Indo-Canadian stage and television. In the television series she has been producing weekly for the last 9 years, she has covered a wide variety of topics dealing with the arts and literatures of India, and with the aspirations, achievements, and problems of Indo-Canadians in Winnipeg. She has also served as Project Director for PALI (Performing Arts and Literatures of India).

A sense of community has steadily enriched her work, which deals with the intersection of different cultures and the adaptation of ancient traditions to life in new and unfamiliar circumstances. The origin and development of *Sita's Promise* demonstrate this commitment and add to the interest of the play itself. In 1978, Dr. Parameswaran invited a dance instructor from Montreal to help her start the first organized dance instruction group in the Indo-Canadian community.

For the graduation performance of the first group of dance students, she wrote a dance drama which was staged on April 25, 1981, at the Winnipeg Art Gallery Auditorium. *Sita's Promise* integrated dance into a story which links epic India with modern Canada through myth and dance. The exiled Rama, Sita, and Lakshmana—the main characters of the Hindu epic the *Ramayana*—find a wounded Arctic tern that has lost its way during its northern migration. Resolving to take it to its home, they travel north through India to the Himalayas where Jatayu, the sacred eagle, carries them to the tern's home by the shores of the primeval ocean now called Lake Agassiz. The work's title is derived from Sita's response to the native children who dance for her and ask her to stay with them: "I through my people, shall surely come again and shall... sing our songs with all the children of the different lands who make this their home."

As Uma Parameswaran comments in her programme notes for the performance, the story is purely imaginary and its characterization of Rama interpretive, not traditional: "It traces Rama's growth from a narrow preoccupation with codes of kingship to an awareness of what it is to be human to a point where he rises to realize his divine mission; the drama ends with our recognition of Rama as the avatar of Vishnu, the Supreme Essence."

The encounter of different cultures is again the subject of *Trishanku*, a sequence of poems covering twenty years and spoken by various voices. Although individual poems gain resonance through the narrative development of the sequence as a whole, and through their dynamic relation with the other poems, each rewards scrutiny on its own. This is especially true of the powerful poem spoken by Chandrika near the end of *Trishanku*:

> I heard him come in the door
> and straight to the kitchen.
> He had snowflakes in his hair
> and his face was white as any neighbour's
> all blood from it in his burning eyes.
> His boots formed an instant puddle
> as he stood at the kitchen door.
>
> Gangajal, he said, I need Gangajal.

The cry for water of the Ganges has particular meaning for Indo-Canadian readers, but the poem's capacity to move readers of all cultural backgrounds typifies the broad appeal of *Trishanku*.

In a review of the sequence, Tom Wayman pays tribute to its "startling and powerful collage of the experience of uprooting and resettlement, of the intermingling of personal and social histories, and of many other human dimensions involved in transplanting an ancient culture to a new land." Within this context, the range of topics which Dr. Parameswaran treats is far-reaching: childbirth and child-rearing, education, marriage and the family, death, friendship and community, poetry itself. The most striking feature of *Trishanku* is the vivid sense of life created by the memories, dreams, and present reality of each speaker; this convincing characterization and its impact on the reader demonstrate that Uma Parameswaran is well able to meet the challenge posed by the sequence's Invocation:

> Begin with the world that is
> Though the worlds that were
> And worlds that will be
> Clamour and hammer
> to enter.
>
> Begin with one,
> Anyone, but make him truly him
> And thereby you, and your people
> And thereby us.

Winnipeg
8th February, 1990

(JUDITH KEARNS)

Dr. Judith Kearns is editing an anthology of South Asian Canadian Literature for Toronto South Asian Review.

The Door I Shut Behind Me

The Door I Shut Behind Me 3

The light behind the 'No Smoking—Fasten Seat Belt' sign faded. The trans-Atlantic jetliner tore through dense white clouds into the serene blue of the upper sky. Far below, the clouds thinned out into wisps of cotton candy, and the azure of the sky touched the deeper blue of the ocean on which occasional specks trailed streaks of white. Then there were no more clouds, no more darting streaks, only an unfathomable blue below, above, around.

Chander blinked the glare away and focussed his eyes on the book in his hand. The black of the title, the motley orange-yellow-green of the jacket resolved from their hazy halations into a clear spectrum of colours and forms—The Ramayana, a new English translation. His mother had given this and Annie Besant's translation of the Bhagavad Gita to him at the airport half-apologetically, half-beseechingly, choosing the last hour so that he would not have the heart to refuse. "Keep it on your table," she had whispered, hastily stepping back lest her heart-throbs spurt out of her eyes. She was an undemonstrative, non-interfering mother, and this was the nearest she had ever come to imposing anything on him. She left it to that single moment and gesture to tell him of her prayers for his safety and her hope that he will turn, occasionally at least, to the wisdom and solace contained in these books.

Chander had made an equally idealistic gesture to himself. On the way to the airport he had stopped the car at a bookstore on Mount Road to get 'some reading matter for the journey' as he sheepishly told his parents: what he had bought was a copy of Chandrasekhar's *Radiative Transfer*. It was not his field of study, nor was it one that would or could be read during a journey. Yet, as the car sped him through his last miles on Indian soil, he had felt an urge to hold that book. To see it was to think of its Indian-born author, and to think of him was to open a world of ambition and inspiration.

"Hullo! I am Kishen Agrawal."

Chander looked up at the unctuous-faced young man who exuded friendliness and perfumed hair oil. He half rose from his seat and took the proffered hand. "V.R. Chander," he said in a low voice as though to compensate for the other's crude loudness.

Agrawal sat next to him and started talking about himself. When Chander did not offer corresponding personal details, Agrawal set himself the task of drawing out the information. Chander was annoyed. He disliked the custom of exchanging life stories on sight. However, he was as unaccustomed to evading straight questions as he was to asking them. Reluctantly he submitted to the cross-examination. He was twenty-five years old, had a Ph.D. degree from Madras University, was unmarried, had three brothers and two sisters, one of them married. He had a two year research associateship with the University of M. at an annual salary of $8,500.

"Wonderful! You will stay on, of course?"

"Probably."

"You do have an immigrant visa, I suppose. Canadian Immigration gives it to most fellows who come on a salaried job. Unfortunately, being a student, I don't have that passport to lifelong luxury. Have you calculated how much one can save in three years?" He added up various figures—for food, lodging, income tax, insurance, car, entertainment—and the total savings came to a six figure amount in Indian currency.

As the questions and counselling went on Chander was aware of a growing resentment. He also felt acutely self-conscious each time an air hostess or passenger passed by. Agrawal, insensitive to his own loudness and Chander's discomfort, waxed more friendly and voluble. He spoke mostly about his own achievements, but he interspersed his autobiography with adverse comments on western culture. As the air hostess leaned across to pull out Chander's lunch table he said in Hindi, "Do you see how she sways and leans over? Seductresses all," and he lewdly smacked his lips.

An appetizing aroma of food filled the plane as lunch trays were carried up the aisle. Suddenly Agrawal fell silent, and fidgeted. Chander wondered if he was, perhaps, diffident about the correct use of tableware. Agrawal leaned towards him and asked, "How does the damn flush work?" He jerked his thumb towards the washrooms. Chander wanted to say, "I knew all along that you had a firsthand knowledge of the western way of life." But he softened his sarcasm by saying, "Same as in other planes."

"On the Delhi-London flight I tried all those knobs and faucets but nothing happened. The handle isn't in its usual place. I am a man of regular habits," he went on piteously, "my whole day is upset if I don't start it right. I am feeling ill already." His face was a study in misery. Feeling mean for having teased him, Chander told him where to look for the pedal. But his sympathy was all too shortlived. When Agrawal returned to his seat it was with the words, "Our toilet habits are much cleaner. These westerners..."

The same trend of criticism was carried through the meal. The westerners were far behind in their culinary arts, they had no taste buds, no appreciation for the finer shades of flavour....

Everything about his neighbour revulsed Chander—his shining rayon suit, his ornate watch strap, his plastered hair, his heavy north Indian accent, his egoism, his shallow generalizations. As Agrawal droned on, Chander had a sense of being trapped, a premonition that it was going to be difficult to shake him off.

The premonition proved correct. When they landed Agrawal took the lead, rather efficiently too. They checked in at a hotel downtown; when Chander came out after a shower he found Agrawal on the bed, busily circling ads concerning inexpensive boarding houses. He had bought both the local newspapers, got a map of the city, and information about buses to the university, and a weekly guide to the current entertainment programmes in the city.

"How about going to one of these joints after dinner?" he asked, pointing to an illustrated advertisement of a nightclub. Chander replied that he was not interested. That set Agrawal talking on his favourite topic. It was not yet seven o'clock. Why go to bed so early? And alone too! (Delighted with his joke he repeated it several times.) Surely Chander did not intend turning his back on simple pleasures? Didn't he want to celebrate his arrival? Come on an immigrant visa too! Do in Rome as the Romans do, boy. (Again he was tickled by his wit.) "I wish I had your visa! Boy, are you lucky? Let me see your magic wand." He rifled through the contents of Chander's briefcase and extracted the landing card from the passport. He held it as one would a jewel. Theatricalism was part of Agrawal's personality. He declaimed, "...'evidence that the rightful holder is a landed immigrant...' The magic carpet to health, wealth and happiness—THE GREEN CARD!"

Chander dryly said, "It isn't green, it isn't a card, and this isn't United States."

Agrawal ignored him. "...a treasure to be guarded for ever and aye. Keep it in your wallet." He picked up Chander's wallet and put it in.

Chander stared at the other's thin line of moustache with distaste. Why had he allowed this leech to close in on him? Why had he not parried his questions? walked off to another seat? told him to shut his goddam mouth and go to hell? Was it patience that made him listen to the boor? Was it tolerance that kept him from rebuking? Or was it weakness? Tolerance and weakness—one was considered a virtue, the other a vice, but were they after all different words for the same quality? Was it tolerance that had allowed India to suffer wave after wave of political and cultural invasions? Tolerance that had prompted Hinduism to be so submissive while missionaries and governments had drawn away its people and wealth? Or was it weakness? Non-violence or cowardice? Two nomenclatures for the same quality, and that quality a national trait for a people who flaunted it by using the more flattering name...a nation made of spineless thinkers and unthinking egotists...and the Agrawals always led the Chanders by the nose...because the Chanders permitted them to...

Agrawal was saying, "You ask it, we have it. That is the way the wind blows here. And the peaches you can't get for money you can get with sweet words as you will see on campus..."

Chander stood over the other man's bed. Words stormed their way out, virulent, devastating words. Agrawal was a bundle of preconceptions and prejudices, a shallow, selfish, callow brute, pampered by his illiterate society which adulated university graduates as gods on earth. What a society! Gossipy women who at thirty were already elephantine, with pendulous breasts and flabby abdomens, lazy, debauched men relaxing the afternoons away against dirty bolsters in their fly-infested shops, chewing betel leaves and spitting tobacco juice on the sidewalks below their shops, selling adulterated sweetmeats and shortweight grocery to poor customers whom they further exploited with usurious loans....

Chander stopped, shocked, when Agrawal burst into sobs. Agrawal defiantly spluttered between sobs, "I am a shopkeeper's son. My mother is a gossip, and my wife is fat. My children do play on the street with snotty noses. But I love them, I want them. I would rather have them around me, and me on my ropestrung cot in my dung-polished courtyard than be this...here..." he flailed his hands helplessly against the newspaper sheets that crumpled and rustled under him.

Chander's shocked distaste changed to fascination as he watched the prone figure on the bed crying unashamedly. It dawned on him that he envied this man. He envied him for this experience, this feeling of utter lostness in new surroundings, this surging, tempestuous, irrational onslaught of nostalgia for persons and a place. This man could live a life of discovery because he could be carried away by wonder, could be moved to tears by yearnings. In Chander there was no yearning, there was no wonder at the sight and feel of a civilization so different from his own. At that moment Chander forgave Agrawal for everything realizing that some subconscious feeling of lostness had moved him into attaching himself to a fellow countryman.

"I'd give anything, anything in the world to see one of my own people, to hear my own language," Agrawal was saying. With a shock of short-circuited sympathy Chander realized that Agrawal was not talking of his family, but of his linguistic community. Here they were, two men who came from the same country, saluted the same flag, worshipped the same gods, yet so alien to each other! Was the alienness due to individual differences alone? "My own people, my own language..." Could they never be one people unless they had but one language? Was it, after all, only language that could hold a nation together in peacetime?

Be that as it may, this man needed to see his own people, and to speak his own language. An idea struck him. He reached out for the telephone directory.

"Maybe we could run through a list of names common in your part of the country," he said.

Agrawal jumped up. "Great idea! Let's do that." He unceremoniously grabbed the directory and flipped through the pages, spelling out the names aloud. "No, no Agarwal or Agrawal, no Panday or Pande or Pandya... Shrivastava, here is one, Shrivastava, Manohar K. Sunset2-6309, what is that, Sunset?"

Chander explained, and Agrawal went to the phone. The ensuing conversation was loud and cheerful at both ends of the line, Shrivastava was just starting out for the Mundhras' home; they had an informal get-together of Indians on the first Saturday of every month; Agrawal and his friend were most welcome, he would come by in ten minutes and pick them up; hadn't they dined yet? they'd get used to early dinners in this country...no matter, Mrs. Mundhra will surely have something...

Agrawal was excited. He plastered down his hair and reknotted his tie. He scooped out his clothes from his suitcase and pulled out a stack of phonograph records from the bottom. He pulled out a bag of small packets. "I must take these. Betel leaves are to us as LSD is to Ginsman eh? These are dehydrated and powdered, isn't that great?" He emptied more than half the contents into his coat pockets.

"That's a lot to take," Chander said.

"Poor guys, they haven't tasted it in years, I bet."

Chander felt a twinge of guilt. He had brought two pounds of scented and spiced areca nuts, but he did not want to share it with anyone. Suddenly he knew what he envied in Agrawal. Spontaneity. That was it. Spontaneous nostalgia, fellow-feeling, generosity.

At the Mundhras' Agrawal greeted everyone with warm enthusiasm. Chander could not. As always, he shrank into himself in company. He had always attributed the withdrawal to sensitivity, but now, still in the mood of reassessing values, he accused himself of innate snobbishness. I am the insensitive one, he reflected, a clod that cannot respond or be touched by any strong emotion.

Mrs. Mundhra, a smiling, sweetfaced woman with several rungs of fat showing at the waist, served them a meal of sorts.

Then they joined the twenty odd persons in the large living room. Chander, somewhat thawed out of his aloofness, was handed over from person to person, all of whom asked the same questions about his work and gave the same assurances on the friendliness of the people and related the same jokes about the winter ahead.

Within minutes Agrawal had become part of the company. Chander noted that he did not use his native Hindi very long. There were people from different parts of India, and everyone spoke only English. Even the children who came in from the adjoining room spoke English. At first Chander instinctively shied away from the twang and accent in the children's speech; he was being as absurd, he told himself, as the interpreter at the embassy in France who resigned his job because even the local children spoke better French that he did. Rationalising did not assuage the hurt that Chander felt at being told that the children spoke no other language. The lady he questioned replied, "...my baby's first words were in our Marathi—Aai Dada—but once I started taking her out to the park it became "Mommy-Daddy", and now she doesn't even understand Marathi."

A man next to her said, "Just you wait a few years and she will be correcting your English! My ten-year-old daughter is on tenterhooks whenever her friends drop in; she is afraid we'll say or do something wrong."

They spoke with complacent pride.

In India Indians built walls of 'My people, my language' between themselves. Here Indians apparently could not care less whether their children had any knowledge or feeling about their country, religion and language. Slowly the implications of their immigrant status dawned on him. Till now he had thought of his visa only as an unwanted and tedious formality, a wasteful trip to Delhi for a personal interview at the High Commission which had lasted less than ten minutes, and had consisted solely of questions that he had already answered on the printed forms. Now, he gathered from others' experiences that it was a precious document that many of their acquaintances had not succeeded in obtaining. They narrated the stories with the smugness of people who had 'arrived' talking sympathetically of those who had not made it.

With increasing bewilderment and hurt Chander noted their attitudes.

Someone asked him if conditions in India were really bad. Conversation stopped and everyone waited for his reply. Just as he started telling them about the drought, one of the women chipped in to tell him in detail about the thousand dollars they had collected last year for the soldiers. She spoke in a gushy manner of 'the girls who worked so hard', and of the dinner and folk dances they had arranged. Chander was annoyed that the Indo-Chinese war should have been no more to her than an occasion for a social venture. But the others seemed to enjoy her loquaciousness. Chander then spoke of the long queues everywhere, for grain, fuel, milk, medicine... He realized that his audience was being politely sympathetic, as though he was sharing some personal grief which was outside their orbits of interest. Roused to anger by their callous indifference, Chander continued in a higher key of emotion. He spoke of the blackmarketing, the rampant corruption and bribery and inefficiency... He was conscious that he was magnifying their indifference and exaggerating his descriptions, but he felt impelled to provoke them into active sympathy and identification. They were not provoked. They politely changed the topic; once again conversation groups were formed, and Chander found himself in a group that was sorting out Agrawal's records.

"Do you have any Pankaj Mullick records?" someone asked.

Agrawal did not. Another asked for classical recordings. Agrawal drew a blank there too. He had all the latest film hits but no one seemed interested.

"Ah! here is a Saigal album," a young man enthusiastically brandished the record. Several others responded, and in silence everyone heard the first song. Then they spoke of old films. Saigal sang on in the background. There was deep nostalgia in the air.

What astounded Chander was that they spoke of the distant past. The first among them to leave India had left it only ten years ago, yet the India they had in mind was not the India they had left but the India of their boyhood, and often enough not even that. The young man who was jubilant at finding the Saigal album could not have heard or seen Saigal on the silver screen because Saigal was of the 1940's; so that what he recalled was not even his actual boyhood but the dreams of his boyhood. To some of them trams still trundled by on Madras streets, anti-British slogans and processions still rang through the country, and Lala Amarnath's double century against Don Bradman's eleven was still the greatest event in cricket history.

It was not callous indifference that prompted them to be blind and deaf; it was some nostalgic idealism, or was it escapism? They seemed to have an image in mind, a golden age of romanticised memories. They did not even want to experience those pleasures again as was evident when Agrawal passed a plate of his betel packets. They reminisced about the betel-areca shops at the street corners, the vendor dipping into a dozen different tins of spices and liquids to make up the roll of stuffed betel leaf, the roadside Romeos clustered round his little shop..., but only a few took Agrawal's packets.

What were they? Indians or Canadians? They had not changed their food habits; the women had not changed their costume; apparently they were a close-knit ethnic group; still far from being assimilated into the general current of life around them. Yet they were as far from the Indian current. They shied away from talk of their return. They hoped to go back, they said, but Chander felt that their hope was for a time as far in the abstract future as their memory was for an abstract past.

Like the mythological king, Trishanku, they stood suspended between two worlds, unable to enter either, and making a heaven of their own.

Chander felt a great weight within himself. "This smoke-music-voice filled air has given me a headache," he told himself, moving to a corner table and picking up a deck of cards. Mechanically he started a game of solitaire.

But the weight was not in his head. It was in his chest, a thudding, throbbing weight. The throbbing stopped but the weight remained, and also an inexplicable sense of loss, anger and contempt.

Chander pulled out his wallet and looked at the light blue piece of paper on the top left corner of which a crown floated above a shield held by a lion and a unicorn. "This card is required for customs clearance and when making application for citizenship. It will also prove useful for many other purposes." He looked at the words as though they held a threat. The passport to lifelong luxury...the devil's bait to lifelong exile....

He sat very still, staring at the words. He felt a great surge inside him, a swirling, forceful torrent sweeping onwards and dashing furiously against the sluice gates of self-control. For a moment he indulged in the thought of what a relief it would be to let himself be carried away in that current. But years of emotional restraint held their own. "I am distorting things—people and values—out of all proportion; I am being irrational, childish, making an emotional furore over a harmless piece of document, two inches by eight, that holds no more compulsion or threat than my driver's license portends death in an accident." Even so, he could not bring himself to replace that card in his wallet. He was aware that someone was approaching the table. Quickly he continued his game of solitaire. A pale, short man of thirty-five pulled a chair and joined him.

"That is enthralling music," he said, "the album got into Agrawal's collection by mistake, one would think." His voice was surprisingly rich for his small body, and his fingers surprisingly long and slender. Chander watched him beat to the rhythm of the record on the table.

"You read characters fast," Chander said, relaxing.

"He wears his on his sleeve. A bore, but goodhearted. This album must be a recent addition. I thought I had all of Ravi Shankar's recordings."

"This is his latest. Came out a few months ago."

"Beautiful! It is so different from his other records. The sitar is a sad-sounding instrument and Ravi Shankar ... just listen to what the maestro does with it! You can almost hear the anklet bells of dancing women! So different from his usual pathos!"

The music built up towards a crescendo of joy. He continued to soliloquise, "We are a happy people, an innocent people. Our devotional songs are love songs because our god is our lover, not our judge. We do not crawl on our knees to his throne, we dance our way into his arms. We were not meant to suffer and starve. Nor to exploit and deprave each other."

Chander felt a happy kinship with this man. He extended his hand and said, "By the way, I didn't get your name. Mine is Chander."

"I am Harish Bahl."

"Glad to know you. Your name was mentioned earlier, I forget in what connection. Oh yes... er..." Chander's grip loosened instinctively as he remembered.

"Married to a Canadian," Bahl completed gently, withdrawing his hand.

Chander was acutely conscious of the weight again. It was right there, inert, crushing.

Once: Chander was fourteen. It was his first season in an adult cricket team. His eldest brother, Adityan, was the captain. It was the final day in the final match of the tournament. Chander returned to the pavilion after forty minutes of steady batting and twenty-two runs. At three o'clock he had to go home and accompany his grandmother to the temple. When he left the field they needed thirty-five runs to win the match and the trophy. Thirty-five runs to make in ninety minutes with four wickets in hand. It was easy as eating jam.

But when he returned home at half past five, the boy next door hollered to him that they had lost, "thanks to the captain scooping a ball right into the bowler's hands" ten minutes after Chander had left. The other wickets had fallen like ninepins of course.

Chander had run into the house and to his brother's room. In blind anger and disappointment he rushed at his brother, intending to hit him with all his might. But the closed fist did not smite. They fell limply on the older boy's chest and he burst out crying. He buried his face against his brother's shirt where sweat had made a yellow half-moon under the armpit and he sobbed.

That was the last time Chander had cried actual tears. He felt those tears rising again, tears from the depth of some divine despair rising for the second time that evening. But he was not fourteen now, and Bahl was not his brother. Yet, for a moment, hearing that rich voice he had thought, seeing those ascetic eyes he had hoped, holding that firm clasp he had felt... Chander sat very still and stared at the half-finished game of solitaire.

Bahl picked up an issue of *Time* from a side-table and sat down across from him. Though all Chander wanted was to be by himself, he felt self-conscious, constrained to say something. There was always that inane but safe loophole, the weather. "So warm in here, one wouldn't know it is close to freezing outside," he said.

"The first winter is usually quite enjoyable, every day a challenge; it is the second or third winter that gets one down."

"I don't expect to be here that long. I just want to pick up some work-experience and go back home."

"That's what we all say for the first year or two. And then it's too late. One more brain-drain casualty." His eyes moved to Chander's landing card.

That's all right. We can do without you and your like, Chander wanted to hit at him. But at the same time he felt accused and impelled to defend himself. "This is the age of individualism," he said, "and not of abstract ideologies of patriotism and nation-building."

"Absolutely," Bahl said quietly, again more to the open magazine in his hand than to Chander. His voice was like the murmur of breeze on water. "I alone am important, not abstract ideologies of patriotism and nation-building, go piss them away down the rivulets cascading down the Nilgiris where the eucalyptus leaves crackling underfoot spark boyish fancies that flame like the sun's glorious spurt of blood before it sinks behind the blue hills where wafts the smell of coffeeshrubs between which slither silent cobras that raise their hoods to the piper's tune as he puffs his cheeks and contorts his wiry frame at Sulluru station to entertain into coin-throwing the Grand Trunk passengers going north through teaktigerdacoit jungles and the plain where the Ganga flows from the mountains where Himavan rules and Siva dances on snowbound Kailas the dance of joy from which alone doth spring love laughter every worthwhile thing... and I metamorphosed into a hybrid way of life ostrichwise ignore the bonds that break one by one, and grow gray with renown and riches, and children who will never know their lost patrimony or knowing, hold it in contempt."

In the silence that followed, the sounds of the plaintive sitar picked up again, and from the farther recesses and rooms came the buzz of conversation. More briskly Bahl said, "When we leave our country we shut many doors behind us though we are not aware of it at the time."

Chander, willing his hands into steadiness, carefully placed the queen of hearts below the king of spades and said, "There are many doors ahead of us."

Trishanku

Invocation:

Where should I begin?

There was a time
When words came to me
And I strung them
    as my grandmother strung glass beads
    to curtain her doorways,
    tubes, spheroids and decahedrons,
    red, skyblue, yellow and green.
Lovely, lovely, I whispered
Running my fingers
Over bright beads and words
That glittered in the morning sun.

Then came a time
When feelings quietly rose
    as the spring at Alakananda
    rises up from earth's womb
    above distant Badrinath;
And words rose, flowed over,
Swept down carrying rocks and trees
In their tumultuous wave.
Images clustered
    like beehives from the cliffs
    that perilously overhang the Narmada
    at the narrow rapids
    where the boatman carefully rows
    along the rocky path
    between gushing waters
    and the marble wall.

But now all is turned inside out,
language and feelings.
I see the monsoon rain pour down
  like needlejets from showerhead;
The blue-white glaciers of Athabasca
Remind me of calendar pictures;
And the pain etched on the woman's face
As she coaxes the smoking wood to flame
While her child moans against noonday pangs

Recalls a scene in a Satyajit film.

Where then shall I begin?

* * *

Begin with his name—
Vyasa's scribe—
Who gives clear sight
And clear vision.
Om Ganesaya Namaha.

Begin with one
Not with many.

Begin with A
And words will follow.

Begin with here
Not with there.

Begin with the world that is
Though the worlds that were
And worlds that will be
Clamour and hammer
to enter.

Begin with one,
Anyone, but make him truly him
And thereby you, and your people
And thereby us.

Poet:

"Born under one law, to another bound,"
What will you say of me, Fulke Greville,
To me or for me
Who was born under two laws and bound
To a third? I was
In love begot, with love laid
On alien bulrushes to be picked up,
Cared for, adopted,
By my fairy godmother—
Dei Gratia Regina
Of the gem set in the silver sea
Seat of Mars etcetera etcetera—
Who dropped me when she withdrew
As sedately as she could
Wrapping the Union Jack around
Her dismembered strength;
Picked up again by one
Who frowned on cross-breeding black and white
But not the miscegenation of cultures
White and brown.
And what shall I do now, Fulke Greville,
And what?
Shall I hang myself in the sky
As Trishanku did of old?
What new Elect shall I lead
To what Sinai to bring down
What law?

Chander:

The fishermen knew him well,
his rich ready response
to their respectful salutations.
Knew that both
he with his gold bordered turban and goldheaded cane,
they with their bronzed silhouettes and muscles,
belonged to worlds
other than those of city men.

  Loudly they would push and heave and sing
  each catamaran past the bar
  swarthy biceps shimmering in the morning sun.
  Would you want to come, little master,
  they'd say, come with us?
  but you must wait till your wheat-skin
  can bear the sun.

And I, my hands tightening
in grandad's firm lax palm,
would wishmove the boats to their song
until it and they were dark lines
against the frothy green, and silver sky.

Chander:

I was pushing the boats with them,
drenched in ocean spray
singing to the seagulls.
We crossed the breakers and let go.
They turned back for the next boat
and did not see the wave swallow me.

It lashed me down
I saw the sea froth white
saw silver fish snap their tails
saw green algae clustered on the sand
and I heard the deep roar of the ocean bed

and I screamed awake
to feel grandad's hand.

This dream stayed with me for years, growing,
growing till I found an antidote:
I'd tell myself in my dream
"It is only a dream and soon
I shall wade to sand
and land and grandad's hand."

Chander:

When the crab's footprint grew small
and translucent pebbles lost their charm
and the lights from anchored queens
twinkled me to dreams of other shores,
he looked at me and said it was too bad
I'd never know
what it is to work with gold
and spin fine strands
into chains and bracelets
to adorn bridal arms.

And therefore I sailed the seas and came
to this land of endless sky and snow.
So they thought,
not knowing of that other parting
that led to this.

Chander:

Go break, my heart,
What do I care?
    hardly remember you as mine
    gave you so long ago to her
        and kept the empty shrine
        polished and perfumed

   an eunuch dusting the corridors of time
            hoping
        fondly hoping
      she'd give me hers to place therein.
Go break, my heart
I have no tears to spare
for a stranger.

Usha:

they named me Usha
because i was born in that magic hour
when the unseen sun pierces arrows
across the silver sky
as sleep-amorous Earth
opens languorous arms
against still-dreaming shadows.

Dawn, melodious with chants—
Arise Mother Kamakshi
Arise Kausalya's son
Arise O Lord of the Seven Hills
Hear the lowing of cows
and dancing of peacocks
and sonorous music of priests and temple bells
And bless the world that wakens to a new day.

    But in my Grandpa's library
With stained-glass windows and marble figurines
brought from Venice and distant Florence
there hangs a mahogany-framed lithograph
of Aurora, wraithlike,
pale arms trailing a pink robe
while cherubs blow clarion calls
at the eastern sky bathed in pink
and pale orange beams.

Usha:

i was in slothful night,
till you, my princess of dawn,
wakened me, he said.
i had no sweet nothings to say
as my lips first touched the heat of day.

Chander:

My sister writes every few months,
November and April,
thinking I might come for Xmas
or the summer. Short lists, all underlined
or in block letters:
Bring a car, a blue Chev, and if possible
postcards of your Boeing 707.
Later, all the Katy books, Enid Blytons,
magic slates and if possible summer frocks.

My father, in his large scrawl,
writes every week, often ending:
Find yourself a job, Chander, and stay there;
This country is ruled by blackguards.
I see him in his cane-woven recliner
Reading The Hindu first to last
on the stone verandah.
"Blaggards, allofem swindling blaggards."

My mother wrote to me
In Tamil, "Om" centred top of the page:
My dear son, A mother's blessing.
I am glad to know you like your college;
I am sorry to hear you don't like the food;
I am glad to tell you next-door Usha's marriage
is on the sixteenth, by grace of God.
I am sorry your sister scorched her fingers
with Deepavali firecrackers. It is healing.
My son, this is the land where the Ganga flows.
Your father is well. Our blessings. Mother.
Her first letter

and her last.

Usha:

into my dark chamber
    the sun shone thro a crack
      danced madly
        withdrew
          left me
            more alone
              than ever
                  i had been.

Usha:

you are not here, he said,
Yes i am, yes yes, i willed
myself into willing, yes, yes, yes.
But the worm knows.
Gone the urgency.
It crawled out
on its centipede slime.

Chander:

Dave skated with ease
    circle, figure eight, spiral,
    arabesque, salchow, camel spin,
    and landed a perfect axel.
And then with long graceful sweep
he skated up and down
An Inca runner, a Hermes,
hair swept back by wind.

Come, he said, we must go farther,
Northeast beyond the village.
And I stumbled along.
We skated
    past village lights
    past coyote howls
to where the ice was cracking
in thunder beneath us.

This is it, he said
Quite something, eh?
And he moved away.

The stars shimmered above me
The frozen masses roared under,
And I on black glass.

The Door I Shut Behind Me

I saw her in the distance
As I always knew I would
And she looked exactly the way
I always knew she would.
A little older than when she'd stand
on the terrace drying her new-washed hair
long and wavy
            and I below her grandpa's library
        its stained glass windows
    behind me
  taking her in
embracing, absorbing.

Usha, I whispered, at last!
I always knew we'd meet again
always knew we'd come together
at last, at last.

I skimmed across the black sheet
Arms outstretched: Usha.
Stars, sky, village lights, all
all sang with me: Usha.

Dave cut in mercurially from behind me
Yelling above the stars, the sky,
the thunderclaps of ice,
    forcing me to swerve
not a moment too soon
    from the ribbon fence
beyond which
beyond which
  no doubt
      some fluorescent rays from algae
          threw strange shadows.

Chander:

    City of my birth
I come.
    Pollen from treetop blown
    from wintry north and sown
    in fertile tropical earth
I come
    Home to you.

Dry throat unquenched
    by heatcooled translucent cubes
    from frostfree nodownpayment whitewalled smoothness
I come
    to your coconutmilkmotherness
                    waiting for me.

Madras! I love you.
Your broad beach road where the polished tar
Flings mirages that vapour on my speeding car,
Your sands stretched out beside the sea
Where at my feet laps eternity.

Seven months and then

Your sullen sky, your sweltering air,
flashy rich, blind beggar's stare,
    wreck of twenty ruinous years when the sheep
    looked up and were not fed.

Breakers roll.
No Aeneas I, I cannot bear thee.
    I ought, you ought, we ought love
    love toosoonhatebecoming love
    the land where we're born.
I fly super VC 10 that leaves the sound behind—
    louder the thudding guiltshame supersonic roaring
    stern daughter of the voice of god heartpounding—
Back to the land where my sons their roots shall find.

Chander:

He travelled with me.
Mister Satish Mundhra
as he introduced himself
pumping my hand in his *bania* chubbiness.
That said it all; Mister Satish Mundhra.
Sure enough he didn't know how to flush
the toilet in the Boeing 707. Sure enough
he eyed the stewardesses lewdly, looking down
the cleft of their bosom as they leaned over
to serve lunch.
It was so easy to hold him in contempt.
I did, and do,
But
When in our hotel room in Montreal,
where we had to stop overnight,
He cried, tears unashamedly streaming down
his *ghee*-fed cheeks,
"I'd give anything to be back home
on my ropestrung cot under the monsoon sky
in our courtyard plastered
with sweet-smelling cowdung water"
I envied him yes; yes I feared for him
too, my uncouth innocent brother
lured to this land of endless skies.

Chandrika:

Madras! I love you.
Your broad beach road where the polished tar
Flings mirages that vapour on my speeding car,
Your sands stretched out beside the sea
Where at my feet laps Eternity.
Madras, I hope one day to call me your own
Though pledged now to the land
Which my love has made our home.

Ushá:

into my dark chamber
The sun came fiery white.
afraid, i received him
with a prism.
And he scattered a spectrum
Of resplendent hues,
Dazzling
And
Barren.

Usha:

it is nature's way, they said,
To throw out those unfit to see
the light of day.
and they dropped him in a white-lid jar
and carried him away.
Threw him down the incinerator perhaps,
       flames sucking at those unformed lips
         that never will suckle here
My son, heir to the heritage of the solar kings.

Dilip:

Amma, I like school.
It is such fun.
We play most of the time
And sing songs in French.
Amma, fingerpainting is such fun
So many bright bright colours
And we can use all we want.
Amma, if a crayon breaks
You can just throw it away
And take a new one!
Ma, you think you could change my name
To Jim or David or something?
Amma I love recess time.
Did you see the tyres?
The tyres tied together?
And you can climb up
and sit inside and swing?
Such fun!
When the snow comes, Ma,
I'll get less brown won't I?
It would be nice to be white,
    more like everyone else
    you know?
I can do everything on the jungle-gym
That Petey can. I'll show you Saturday.
No school on Saturdays.
Just think, Amma, no school
Ever on Saturdays!
Except that it isn't so good
When you like school, you know?

Sharad:

In our ancestral home
Every newmoon day
Father, as his father before him,
>   in silk dhoti
>   vibhuti on forehead and chest
>   sacred thread dipped in turmeric
sat on a wooden plank
facing the east
>   to repeat the purohit's chant
>   sprinkle holy water with darbha grass
>   and call upon our ancestors.

But here the sun rises southeast
And the planets are all a-kilter,
And all my words questions.

Savitri:

Someone had scared the sun,
Its hairs stood on end.
The green sunflower brightly
blinked black anthers
into an orange sky.
Susie stood on the careening lawn
Bow-legged, snake coiled arms
Stretching to the chimney.
"And this is me grown tall
as Mom going to the Safeway."
The crayons went to work overtime.
Curlers, lipstick on lips on cheek,
breasts popping out of shift.

Savitri:

Horror stared out of Susie's eyes
coursing iridescent tears down
her mudstained cheeks.
Her tricycle lay on its side
its left wheel hugging a Barbie
stretching out her hand to her severed head.

I swept Susie into my arms
where the great sobs hiccupped
incoherently into silence.
It is only a toy, baby, I said,
only a little doll, my darling,
only plastic moulded into human form.

Carrying her in, I saw Peter,
Pale lips set tight in pain
and humiliation walking to the door.
Susie's mother was dialling
a date with the other man
Whose name who knows and why?
She picked them up and dropped them.
Peter is only a man, neighbour,
only a man who was fun till now.

Jayant:

Distance makes the heart grow fonder,
to hand a cliché to you
my sententious dad.
But Jeesus face it
It is a sprawling shambles
passed down untouched
from the days of the Peshwas.
A half-mile walk to the shithouse
      and pigs slurping
one man's poison is another's food
Jeez.

Bihari:

Jes lookit these womens
nekkid almost as god made them
Why my *chaddi* has more cloth
than their whole dress!
   Shame shame
   What she-dogs they be.

Savitri:

Hands.
Reaching out from every which where.
Some hands...now needing mine
now steadying.
But distinctions blur,
Whose the need
Whose the reassurance?

Little Pete Korolski
   abandoned child
   of foster homes
   and bright eyes
blinking back tears
as he ushered parents
with grave ritual
pair by pair.

But why does my hand
linger on his shoulder?
His need?
   or is it mine?

Jay-Jyoti-Krish
My children who grow, have grown
Within me kicking and butting,
diapers, woollies, ballet,
junior league,

Grow, are growing, have grown,
Grew, were growing, had grown,
Present perfect, past continuous
etcetera

But these my children
Twenty four of them always
And always nine years old.
Little Markandeyas
whose faces change
and names
    always mine
and mine for nine months
of one year.

And I, Pluton,
reach out for them
Yearning to gift them
my silence, my dark warmth
that they might carry me
a still core as they stretch
towards the light of day.

Usha:

early this morning my son sped away from me.
My womb wakened me with gurgles of pain,
soundless farewells to him who would not stay
And I woke to feel him twisting his way out
slowly   wrenchingly   silently
Then, opening the door, he slid swiftly down
gelatinous halls

    he has a way
    of torrenting out
    I cannot reconcile me to,
    a breathless rush to vapour
    into the Infinite
Leaving me bleeding barren tears.

Mystic, ecstatic, desperate is this cycle.
The first days when my womb feels
              though I only know
he is come, and tucks him into his tubular cradle
rocking him, gently rocking him down.
And I tell myself
    with the cool objectivity of scientific analysis
It will come
    he becomes it, you know how it is
    with dispassionate scientific precision
It, I say, will probably
    law of probability age of computer data
happen this time
Cannot but.

Days.
Then I hear him groping for life and I run
O with what rapturous haste I run to bring
life-giving Ganga to his door.
All is quiet. The sleep of fulfilment.
Nor hope nor need but certainty.
Cannot but
    messy carpets, diaper pails
    burps and blubber

Two weeks.
Then doubt drives placidity as surely as the sun
Shall thaw the Assiniboine.
It is then I take him shopping.
I walk him through Canada's Christmas store
Pointing out toys
    the train sparking swishing on the curving
    ever-curving track,
Hoping, bribing him to stay.
And then I grow desperate
and make rash promises
    as never lover made his love
I promise him the largesse of the earth,
The heritage of the solar kings
and then, feeling a deep fear he does not care
I invoke him, Eternal Lover, Infinite Love,
I beg, plead, supplicate, yes haggle
like a fishwoman that he may stay.

And then, early one morning I waken
to my womb's soundless gurgles of pain....

Dilip:

The thirteen-liner
fat with the spoils of summer
scampered off into a burrow. The weasel
black tip of his tail
like an arrow stopped short
and darted his bright eyes around.
Don't come out
you stupid squirrel, I thought,
knowing they always did, dumb things.

The mustele erminea homed into the hole.

When we were still on Stradbrook, Father would take me along the Park trails, with binoculars and breathholding excitement, and tell me stories of how the chipmunk got its three stripes from Rama's stroking fingers at the time they built the bridge to Lanka; once we saw a star-nosed mole, its twenty two pink tentacles lying like a flower on its snout.

Dilip:

Father,
your other sons
are making it in a big way.

Can't you
let go of me
let me be only what I can be?

I don't want to learn golf
or squash or go to SJR or Medical School
or into Computers even though you've bought
            me an Apple
when it is still thought a fruit.

I am just a B or B+ guy;
your ambitions, Mother's pleas,
nothing can push up my grades any.

Sharad:

Who are these faceless people
among whom my life is oozing away?
Each is so self-contained
    glancing, swiftly but completely
    through me:
               why are you here?
And the bus moves on, and we.

Poornima:

I keep a water tray in my yard
For the birds that live in the thicket
Beyond our wall.
        Thoreau would have approved
And Audubon.

I hear them chirping
Tweeting, hooting, calling, whistling
In the thicket
Beyond our wall.

I have yet to see at my trough
Any bird but sparrow.
Here is one, a male,
Grey pincushion on his throat.
He dips his beak,
One wing, then the other,
Shakes thimself,
Lifts his tail ever so little
Leaves a black dropping
With a white head.

Chander:

Please draw me a planetarium projector
My ten-year-old poring over homework says.
"The Brittanica, boy, always the Brittanica first."
But I reach out for my 1962 Collier's,
my first acquisition, it still smells
of my Princeton attic I swear, and pull out
volume nineteen.   She fell out of Pleaides,
edges already fading against the halo
of cheap studio effects,
long wavy hair, eyes looking above camera,
a trait she had.

But it was Saturn that ruled her destiny,
she said, keep away.

The stars are such handy excuses.

But why am I bitter?
My name known to all—
    scientist, professor, community leader,
    school trustee, once Dean, once Head,
    titles I've donned and shrugged off at will
    from the universe that revolves around me.

But the fourth dimension pounces from everywhichwhere
Memories like expanding lacunae in interstellar space.

Chander:

Reporters crowded around as I walked towards the Centennial escalators. TV and newspaper boys.

> How long have you been teaching?
> How do you feel about the Science Symposium idea?
> What made you take the initiative to bring your Indian kids here?
> Do you think more money should be put into country schools?
> Do you think country kids can ever do as well as city kids?

I answered them with the right mix of compliments and complaints. Yes, I've been enthusiastic about it since its inception. Sunil's vision, real decent chap. Yes country kids have it tough. I didn't say they'd be better off concentrating on farming or hunting or whatever it is they do out there. Yes kids are great at innovation. Yes.

I edged out, gratified of course at the spotlight but peeved that it was for being a ruddy judge at this ruddy Symp. and not for my research.

And then this fellow comes along with a troop of natives behind him and they, and I, realized they had the wrong chap. The fanfare was for him, it turned out, a schoolteacher from Long Plain, some Kesavan, all Adam's apple and close cropped hair, wearing trousers that'd been the style in Bombay ten years ago I'd swear. He is probably the same height as I but of course it was his brown skin. Y'can bet they can't make out one brown man from another.

I don't grudge him the tom-tom and honor roll though. Poor chap, has apparently been at Indian reserves for seven years slaving to get the blighters put together something half decent. Sure we've got to encourage the native kids. Probably a put-up job though, the poor sucker must have done it all himself.

Dilip:

Eightnineten years ago we'd walk from Stradbrook
Father and I, to see the floes float by
and watch the migrant gulls far above;
the strongest lead the way, he'd say,
explaining the v. And in the winter
he'd walk on the water, my father.

Now the Red flows by our backyard,
and Father, two weekends early May
and late August, trails the Evinrude III
to the cottage so it can be all summer
at the dock to others' envy.

Chandrika:

"Mexico City! How marvellous!"

"I'm so glad you can go, Mrs. Chander, (everyone in his department pronounced it Chandler without the l) you deserve some time away from the children (it never ceased to amaze them that we had four) and the kitchen."

"Just the two of you. A real vacation." Would anyone understand that a vacation with children is no vacation?

Savitri is the one behind it all. It is only for a week, she said, don't be a worrywart, ladybird. Your house won't burn down. Your children will be right here, under my wing. I'm used to having twenty plus all day, remember? And as for repaying me, I'm sure you'll do it for someone else when the need arises.

She didn't say it all at once, no, we are not ones to make little declamations. Write us a story, she said, the way you used to in the Sunday *Hindu,* long before I knew you. (Ram Rama, that was eons go and for the Children's Corner; I don't even write letters any more, now that the children have taken over family correspondence. Just to Mother once in a long while. In Tamil, so she knows we still speak it at home, though listening to the children no one would believe it.)

Chandrika:

Why are you so silent, brother,
Who in days gone by
delighted us with rich resonance?

> I mourn my chained brothers
> Shut away from sun and air
> Whose voices once chorused with mine.
> I mourn my brothers
> Chained in slavery whose voices
> never loud, are muted now.
> I mourn my brothers who,
> Seduced by false reasoning,
> Accept and spread their lady's creed.

What will you do now, brother,
Who in happier days
Crossed swords with one and all
To hone your skills?
And flailed words into bleeding tears of sympathy?

> Across the seas is a land
> Where man may stand tall
> May walk and talk without fear
> May pray and play in freedom.

I have been to that land, my brother.
It is a good land
Where one can be honest and free,
Can work hard and reap the fruits thereof.
But it is not the land for you and me.

Let those go there who would be cradled
In soft ease.
Let even those go there
Whose pursuits are of the mind and soul.
Who, free of mundane worries,
Would, in the quiet of books or contemplation
Seek the face of God.

I have been there, my brother,
The land is green but my heart was barren,
Warm are the people but my heart was lonely,
Money flows in rivers but my heart was dry.
Bereft of want and tensions
Bereft of sorrow and pain
Bereft of comradeship
My heart lost its voice, my brother.
It is not the land for you and me.

Chandrika:

On meeting some VIPs at a party

This is no place for stuffed shirts, fellow guests,
   this hospitable room
   where malakite plaques
   from Teotihuacan
   echo the timeless tunes
   of Ravi Shankar's sitar
   while our host pours out your third glass of scotch.
Relax.
Take off your slushy arrogance
   (The rains, by your lady's grace, are on time.)
Loosen your forced loyalties
   (The leash, by your lady's grace, is long.)
Hang up your coat so heavy with favors and pardons
For we need none of these in this hospitable room
   where malakite plaques from Teotihuacan
   echo the timeless notes of Raga Mallar.
Back in our native land, my cousins
Stand at your door with joined palms
   (Dead is Aswattama
                the elephant.)*
Back in our native land, my brothers
Have vanished from your sight
Or from ours.

Here pause a moment, my fellow guests.
If my brothers and I
do not shake hands with you
   (though your palms by your lady's grace, are clean.)
Know it is by our will, not yours.

---

* "Dead is Aswattama! the elephant": Knowing that only the death of his son, Aswattama, would impel Drona to lay down his arms, Dharmaputra uttered this cry, adding "the elephant" under his breath as a salve to his conscience.

Chander:

The miles of Hilton plush, once red waves
    rearing to lash me down,
Is now shimmering sand whereon
    I glide my sensuous sole.
With ease I spill platitudes, hedge questions,
    rattle anecdotes,
And with ease
    move among self-contained bubbles of people
    that once left me a gasping shell
    at receding tide.

I am even slowly mastering
The subtler touches of an actor's trade—
The right measure of pause at the right place,
"Hullo" in the right tone to the right face.
    Sudden the bubble pops
    Through the unfinished drink,
    Do I really think
    I can tear away that mask at will?

And then your words touched me
As applause never can—
That elemental touch
Of souls holding hands.

And now I know
My face is still there
Underneath that mask.

Tara:

Namaste! Savitri behn, come in.
So good you are, behn,
looking me up so often
if all is well.
Seat your good self.
Yes, we got vacuum cleaner,
It is so convenient, no?
You phoned yesterday? O I am so sorry
I was not being here.
I will tell you the story, behn,
But first seat your good self.
There, I've put off stove. Let us sit.
It happened this way.
That good lady in next flat
she was going to food store
the Italian one no? on the big street?
And our India store so close
So I am also going.
I buy some vegetables, bhindi and fresh brinjals,
and then I go to join her at her store
The stink hits my nose, but I keep my face
From showing no?
And then I look for her.
Toba toba behn, whole hunks
of animals hanging from hook
like we hang bananas no?
Ram re Ram, my stomach churns
And I rush out.
You too laughing, Savitri behn?
He too is laughing when I tell him.
I have a lot to learn he is telling.
Let me boil some tea, yes yes behn you must.
Your are so kind no?
like my own cousin sister you are being.
But behn, is hard for me to ispeak Ingleesh.

Suri:

Why can't I soo soo on the grass,
Pappaji?
Why do you never let me soo soo?
Not against our garage or appletree,
Not even here off the road.
Miles and miles of bushes and no people
But you won't stop the car.

Jayant:

To each his own hang-up, Dad.
The Pembina strip is no big deal
an aesthetic black hole if you will.
But there's something Jeesus
             that gets to my guts
    from among the eyesore of billboards
         and bald trees
             I feel it
Raring to go up skislopes
    even if only a Stanfield brief
         to hold me up
and Cougar boots that centrally heat
my soul.

Chander:

About to bike off our driveway into the lane,
I see them, in a row
Three kids, seven years old maybe
Or eight, peeing on old Bob's fence.

I stop
   not wishing to interrupt the flow
of their talk.
"I told you it's fun." The accent
is unmistakable Delhi.
"Think ours'll be yellow on the snow?"
"Like dogs'?" They are excited.

"I can draw a circle," he boasts,
the black-haired one,
walking ahead of the redheads.

I probe my own eight-year-old
for the goings on
but he tells me nothing
except that Suri is a great guy
a born leader though he'd come
just in April.

Listen kid, I want to say,
On the alleyside of grandad's house
we'd compete for who could pee farthest.
Damo usually won
Son of a gun he had the longest pistol
we'd ever seen.

Dilip:

For its crazy August
1978 will be on record
in Winnipeg's Guinness book.

On the eleventh it was 95°
And it felt like a hundred and ten.
We had thirty friends in our pool all day.

Chander:

Crossing Main at Portage
after several months in Edmonton
I saw there was no sidewalk.
They had done it, after all,
the city fathers
in defiance of good sense.

I walked down to the Concourse,
hum of ventilation
new smell of Hades.

She was far to the right.

My chest thudded insanely:
It could not be.
I recalled the lake, the stars,
the sky,   and she
sixteen years ago.
And the real she another three.

She paused and asked a tall man,
for directions, I suppose.
And raised her neck and smiled,
Thank you, I suppose.
But that statuesque moment
Pushed all my blood to groin
As it had a hundred times
in adolescence. I paused.
Stand still. Breathe deep. Count to ten,
Till the blood retract.

Nineteen years.
Yet the dream had not died.
A wife of fifteen years, and four children,
Yet passion had not died.
And that
    ridiculous
    perpendicular
    thrust at the sight
    of a stranger
    whose hair happened
    to be long and wavy.

Tara's mother-in-law:

What kind of place you've brought me to, Son?
Where the windows are always closed
And the front door it is always locked?
And no *rangoli* designs on porch steps
To say please come in?
How you can expect Lakshmi to come, son?
You think she'll care to enter
Where the same air goes round and round?
She 'the lotus-seated consort
   of him who reposes
   on the primeval ocean of milk?"
You think they'll bless this food
   three days old
   you store in cans and ice-cupboard?

Son, son, it gives me great joy
to see you so well settled,
children and wife and all
Though my hairs do stand on end
When your wife holds hands with men
And you with other men's wives.
But I am glad, son, I really am
That you are settled good good
And thought to bring me all the way
To see this lovely house and car and all.

But I cannot breathe this stale air
With yesterday's cooking smells
going round and round.
Son, cooking is an every day thing
Not a Sunday work alone
And son, cooking should smell good
The leaping aromas
   of turmeric and green coriander,
   and mustard seeds popped in hot oil
that flavour food, not stink up the air.

Open the windows, son.

I am too used to the sounds
   of living things;
Of birds in the morning
Of rain and wind at night,
Not the drone of furnace fan
   and hiss of hot blasts
   and whoosh whoosh of washing machine.

Open the windows, son,
And let me go back
   to sun and air
   and sweat and even flies and all
But not this, not this.

Chander:

Please pick up party ice and Coke on your way home, was the message on my door in the Secretary's neat hand.

O no, I remembered, it was one of those evenings, Chandri and her one-man campaign to orient newcomers to Winnipeg.

I called Dave and cancelled the squash hour we'd set up for five o'clock.

Newcomers from India whom Chandri carried around like an Aeneas until they settled down and forgot us altogether. My Chandri, god bless her boyscout heart.

There were three couples and countless children. Mercifully, Chandri always sent them to the basement and kept them there, the noisy brats. Unbelievable how noisy kids from India are. I went through the rites, sure enough one of the men wouldn't drink; that's the way it is, you come home Friday evening all ready for a shot and the game on TV, and you find abstemious dinnerguests waiting.

I went through the rites as I said. Found out that one was an Amar Ghose from Jadavpur who knew my work, decent guy; another was Kesavan, from Madras Tech I gathered but he seemed to have been out in the boondocks somewhere—I didn't ask outright, some of these chaps are sensitive as asthmatics to pollen—and the third was someone whose name I couldn't get but didn't care if I never knew, one of those bounders who talk endlessly and in a pseudo-Oxford accent mostly about themselves. And what got my goat was that none of them was directly from India; sure they were new to Winnipeg but old pros at living in the west. There was some point to Chandri putting me through this drag if we were really helping someone find their way but what a waste of an evening making polite talk. To make things worse, I feld a cad when Kesavan told me we'd met at the Science Symposium back in '75.

I saw her when I went into the kitchen for a refill of the ice bucket. I should have seen her earlier, of course, since I'd opened the door for each before the women made a beeline for the family room.

She smiled, noncommittally.

I rushed to my study and closed the door. Stand still. Breathe deep. Count to ten.

The insane throbbing subsided.

Practicality. Should I recognize her? That was the rational thing to do. Be breezy? Well, if it isn't little Usha from next door whom I've known from our knicker days. Or melodramatic? My long-lost love who haunts my dreams! Or a polite Yes of course we were neighbours in Mylapore.

I came out still tonguetied, and slipped furtively into the living room. Like a bloodless thief in my own house.

My wife said it instead. Usha tells me you were neighbours in Madras. You'll have much to talk about. Isn't it a coincidence that Mr. Kesavan was a neighbour of my Uncle Sambu? They've moved to Winnipeg for their daughter Poornima, remember? My tactful Chandri, reminding me I had been briefed.

It is a pleasant surprise, Usha said. But I've been away so long, I left Madras in '62, I doubt we shall have much to talk about.

So that's the way it was to be.

Chandrika:

Twenty hours a week, I thought,
was surely something I should give
my people
now that the children
were at school all day.

It was satisfying at first
To drive them back and forth,
Shop for apartment, furniture,
kitchen things, winter clothes;
a wooden stake and stocking bands
to withstand the first winter's winds.

Lovely the clematis
Against our trellised wall.

And then I found people
who needed more
than apartments, winter clothes.

They are with me all the time
Twice twenty hours each day
My people.
But there is so little I can do
that anyone can do
alone.

They are with me everywhere
As I shampoo my Sita's tresses
I see Harjit
pinned to locker floor
by four of his schoolmates
while the fifth lopped off his hair.

Trishanku 71

As my Mohan
whacks mosquitoes off his bronzed back
I see the welts on Pritam's
bruised by a drunken father.
Was drink the cause
or the result
of his joblessness?

Hasina, new bride from India
Of one who lives common law
with Maria mother of three
two his.

Bihari, driven to suicide
in his basement bachelor suite
of six years.

Lata, caught between love
for her half-wit daughter
secreted away at an Ontario school,
And her husband's steel egotism
that wants no sign of his genetic flaw.

Tara's mother homesick for open windows
encaged until the baby grows up
or Tara quits work.

My heart can hold them everyone
but not my head, which clamours
at the futility of it all.

And nearer home
Usha's daughter now blind
wasting away like the moon
of an incurable and
many-tentacled disease.

Chander:

By dying sudden one night, Mother,
You thought to spare me the agony
Of a long, slow death.
There were no premonitions, no tell-tale spasms
Auguring the end of Spring's ecstasy,
No warning you'd be launched on the river
Which must flow down to the sea.
There was no doctor quietly studying charts
And turning with a professional smile,
"Let us bring this runaway horse to book."
Later, with bedside voice and look,
"Nothing that drugs and diet cannot set right."
And later still, professional quips,
"She'll live to eighty, despite me and you."
Then, with quiet cheer,
"Here's a new drug, new breakthroughs near."
New icons raised to brook the flow
Of the river to the sea.
There were no brief interludes,
When all seemed as before,
And we laughed and worked and dreamed,
Almost forgetting that the river
Inexorably flows to the sea.
There was no desperate turning to the old gods,
No climbing up the seven hills.
And down again to where He rests serene,
Then into every roadside shrine
Hoping to stay the stream
From flowing to the sea.
There was no transfer to the terminal ward
When I clung and cried
And stretched my hand for yours.
By dying in one short night, Mother,
You spared me all this pain.
But not for long.
I burn in the hold
Of a slow, slow death.

Usha:

A river meandering motherly through the plain
my children wading in my placid waters.
I felt your steel feet planted astride my limbs,
felt my waters rise in the catchment of your cofferdam
as you reared your wall to enfold me.

> Did you think, my love, you could hold me
> in the matted coils of your hair
> and funnel me out as and when you pleased?

With a sudden shower that truant boy opened
the floodgates of desire, swept my unleashed waters
on your unready bosom, and then ran away,
trilling his flute, into the winter fog.

> Did I think, my love, I could
> straighten the buckled-in pillars
> of your spans to receive
> my awakened tides?

Arise, my love, for out of the battered foam of my waters,
> out of the pulverized stone of your loins
> he has forged his song:

Rejoice, for though I am gone, the imprint of my hand
> is on this crumbled wall and on these hungry waters
> bound each to each through me.

Rejoice, that the fields you fed may draw
> new strength from your embraces.

Savitri:

It scares me, this other world
that intrudes on me
of a sudden
in everyday actions—
>lifting chalk stick to blackboard
>kettle over teacup
>at intersections, where amber
>turns to red for all but me.

A deer nimbly running towards the lake
but breaking of a sudden, sensing a tiger near.
Then moving forward again
driven
>not by its parching thirst
>but by a sense of inevitability.

Kalidasa must have described it somewhere
for they had a way, the old masters, of
soldering breathtaking tenderness with
nightmarish violence.

Poet:

How I Arrived

There was a time I wrote of marble veined
rocks chiselled by the singing waters of my native
Narmada, of rowing across the summer lake watching
waterbirds wheeling just above, of teethchattering
winter morns when we trailed our elders to the
velvetbug-dotted field to squint through telescopes
at the tailed star streaming in the sky.
   And they said, Right on, you'll make it
someday. But don't imitate.

Then I wrote of first love along the singing
waters of my native river when we wooed each
other with words   walking   winging   warbling,
and in our separate beds lay dreaming of hands
that were yet to touch
and of the golden arch across the monsoon sky
that awaited us at break of day.
   And they said, Right on, somewhat gushy
but you'll make it yet. Don't alliterate.

Then, because I knew what it is to hold the
world in my arms, to see the dancing universe
in the sleepopen caramelsticky mouth of my child,
to be a *gopi* among neat rows of earthen pots,
each condiment in place, the fire put out for the day,
lamp lit for evensong,   I wrote nothing at all,
   Wake up, they said, don't vegetate.

So I wrote again. Of children wading
in the singing waters of the Narmada,
and of *gopis* churning butter in Brindavan.
   No way, they said, go out into the world
before it is too late.

And so I went into the slums
and bathed scabs off newborns, lice off girls' hair
distributed condoms to men who used them on whores,
milk to mothers who sold it to the teashop

down the lane; lived through two epidemics
helping them lay out their dead
but fled
fearing contagion
when election diseases flamed corruption
through the dry land where once the waters
of the Narmada had sung their way to the sea.

Right on, they cried, you've almost made it.
It is there, all but the missing dimension
Of experienced lust. Don't hesitate.

So I walked the streets and wrote
Of flamboyant lusts, nubile erections behind public latrines,
young men flaunting sixshooters, old men
proving to themselves they still could,
postures picked up from Vatsyayana
and descriptions from drugstore novelettes.

You've made it, they shouted, we always
knew you would.

Chaman Lal Dwivedi:

I am Chaman Lal Dwivedi.
Learned in three Vedas
though my name says two,
I made my sons send for me.
What else are sons for?
I have a green card for America
and am also landed immigrant here.
Everything is possible if you know how.
I give lectures on philosophy
   and in languages.
Though I never stepped into college
   being third class matriculate
I am called now to talk to students,
   white men. True worth will tell.

Everything is fine here.
One must make adjustments
of course. At first
I thought this was rakshasa land
where everything is opposite—
where people monstrously huge
make night day
and sleep till noon.
Where women chase men,
like Surpanaka of old.

It was difficult at first
to eat meat and drink liquor—
But the rishis did both
in older days; *sruti,* word of God,
unchangeable, *smriti,* customs
that society accretes and sheds
for change of times.
I, well versed in both, know this,
for I am Chamal Lal Dwivedi
learned in the Vedas.

Savitri:

This sadness that veils your eyes
This silence louder than your ghettoblaster,
When did you get it, my child,
And why?
Conceived in the floodtide of my love
reared in the springtime of my wealth
When   did you   get it
        and   why?
And you in the arms of first love.

In your voice I'd hoped to see the flash
that brightens mine even now;
In your voice I'd hoped to hear
the song of the sky
that comes even now
though never so loud
nor often.

Veejala:

I heard about you and Andre.
Right on, Jyoti,
Here's advice for your age
                         your time
Jump into bed
   do all you want
   wallow
      in the lazy hungers
         of the skin

or
   elephant trunk bearing down
   and lifting through space,
   a ravishing flight pardon the pun
   to its ornate howdah.

But not no way into matrimony.
Jyo, not that.

I born in another age
           another land
know marriage is for keeps
and so can claw back
           shout down
to kingdom come.
but not for you
   that security
   natural as earth to seed.

Poornima:

The green-gold of prairie fields was mine
Till Spring.
And mine the brilliant blue of my mother's lakes.
I delighted in the lady-bug's black wing
And the turquoise hidden in the down of birds.
Bright orange was the factory's spurting flame
And auburn the roof of my brother's barns.
Till Spring.

A sudden thaw broke all resisting banks
And burst the floodway of my sight.

But the murmur of wind amid cedar and pine was mine
In early Spring,
And mine the music of books and rain and splashing cars.
Freely my visions raced across the prairie blue
With meadow larks, sailboats, skateboards skidding through.

Lysol, i.v.'s and intercoms,
Pneumatic wheels gliding along narrow halls.
Needles, distant whispers of pain shushed to sleep;
And then my dreams lay in prairie grass.

My eternal summer shall not fade
In the halls of my father's home
Where my fancies shall freely race
Across fields of prairie gold.

Vithal:

Look, you guys, we've gotta show them,
Yeah, show the bastards we've as much
right as anyone who's come here
in the last three hundred years.
Yeah, show the sonsobitches that we
stand together, and they ain't gonna
divide and rule
no more.

Vithal:

We shall build our temple
where the Red meets the Assiniboine.
Let us swear to stand together
And there can be no fall.
Those pissed off whites can hang a moon.
Yeah that's where their energy lies
Not in their head.

Jayant:

You are way out, Vithal, man.
What do we have in common, Jeesus,
We and those unlettered louts
with their garlic masalas
and unwashed beards?

Vithal:

We shall build our temple
Here where the Assiniboine
Flows into the Red.
And I shall bring Ganga,
As Bhagiratha did of old,
To our land
          our Assiniboine
And the fluteplayer
Dark as *kaya* blossom
Shall dance on the waters of La Salle.

Sharad:

O where is the kusa grass
   where the cleansing Gangajal?
How pick one's way out
   of Abhimanyu's labyrinth?
How bring to surface our forebears'
cumulated *punya* dormant within?

Vithal:

Living like goddam ostriches, we are.
If your house gets stones and eggs
smashed on windows you'd get action
faster from the Defence League
than from any goddam cop.
That's the writing on the wall,
Yeah, that's the fact of life
In this true north strong and free.

Savitri:

Hormones. That's all it is, he said.
You are still rather young
But you now how it is
Early for some, for others late.

    And he held my hand
So I could sit up.
See you next year, same time
same channel, eh?

And I walk out light and free.

    What aunts would give gratis
    My medicare taxes dispense
    with a jargon 15 years dated
    and a two-hour wait.

One can be so sarcastic
When reassured.

Chandrika:

I heard him come in the door
and straight to the kitchen.
He had snowflakes in his hair
And his face was white as any neighbour's
all blood from it in his burning eyes.
His boots formed an instant puddle
as he stood at the kitchen door.

Gangajal, he said, I need Gangajal.

I reached over to the alcove above the fridge
Where I've enshrined our household gods
And took down one of the cupsize copperpots
Sealed at a temple beside the holy river.
His hands were trembling as I placed it there,
And he had snowflakes in his hair.
I'll drive, I said, following to the door
but he patted me absently
as he does our little ones
when they drift into his study.

Ambike, Mother, may he reach in time.

He had not slept for three nights
and his eyes were unseeing,
like those of a ballet dancer poised
to glide above our seeing heads.
I tried to drag him back;
Haven't we got enough parking fines
this week? I said, Let me drop you.
I bent to pull my boots from behind him.
He touched my hair, hands hovering a moment
In my aura.
And then he was gone.

My guts knotted; thus had my father
Touched my head as I kneeled
to touch his feet at parting:
Dheergha Sumangali Bhava.
And my heart rushed out the door

to her who no more would hear those words:
Dheergha Sumangali Bhava.

Ambike, Mother, help her help her help her.

* * *

Gangajal, he said, I need Gangajal
to wash him.

My heart contracted and exploded in fear.
But I reached up to the alcove of our shrine
as I had the day before
and I gave him the last
of my sealed holy water.

Ambike, Mother, may we never miss it
Never need it, never.

Then his words honed in on my ears—
To wash him. Ambike, Mother,
Is *he* about to wash him?
Why you? I burst out, why you?
You haven't recited any slokas
in a hundred years, how can you
play Brahmin now?
I knew it once, he said.

Devi Sureshwari Bhagavati Gange
Tribhuvana Tarini Tara Lata Range
Bhagirati Sukhadayini Matasvata
Jalamahima Nigame Khyataha

It will come back, he said,
All if it will come back.
And he was gone.

* * *

We came together then, all of us,
two hundred and more;
and in the days that followed
there was more love in every home,
more compassion, less grievances
and gripes as each sought comfort
in wedded arms
and held on to those fragile bonds
which are never more hers to hold.

Nor mine.
For the touch of death is on him
and all the waters of the Assiniboine
cannot rub away the smell of darkness
from his arms.

Ambike, Mother,
What ironic hand have you slapped on us
that we should move apart
each from each
for strangers we had seldom met?

Dilip:

Spring is here.
Blackbirds, all male, scarlet flashing
from between their black wings,
flew in from the south last week.
Their mates will follow soon.

I shall go tomorrow to the lake,
clean up the cottage, let sun and air
rid its winter smells of leaves and mould.

I shall walk to the creek
where drakes court with arched neck
and six-beat bobbing of head from side to side;

I shall pick
dark green needles
from newfallen jack pine.

Dilip:

Here in the city
Spring means cankerworms
caterpillars, raking, seeding, bedding.

Summer means mosquitoes
crippled Baygon babies and press scares
and unthinking Malathion raining from the sky.

I shall canoe up and away
from everything that speaks and
endlessly says nothing, radio TV mankind.

Savitri:

"Oh we couldn't possibly celebrate anything this year, least of all a wedding anniversary, even if it is our twentieth."

The pain and reproof in Chandrika's vioce sent a stab through me, a stab that was getting familiar of late. Oh god, how could anyone be jealous of poor Usha who'd had more bad luck than everyone else put together? First daughter, then husband within a year, and miscarriages, "I've lost count of them," she'd once laughed, "same as we can't remember the number of jobs he changed the first five years." Yes, yes, but she had taken away my Chandri and Chander and made a little world of their own, the three of them and their children.

"I sometimes wonder if I shouldn't be jealous of her," Chandri was saying. Startled out of myself, I stared at her. How lovely she was! She had grown beautiful to middle age as happens to so many who start off plain.

She was speaking haltingly, like one thinking aloud. "She seems to have revived something in Chander that he once had...he was so idealistic, so sensitive...almost sentimental.... Time changes everyone, of course, hardens us..even coarsens us...especially here where we lead such self-centered lives...." She rose, as though to put away our coffee mugs but went to the window instead. "It seems a terrible thing to say, Savi, but the anguish of Kesavan's dying and death has been so ...so reassuring...that we still have that core of...what shall I call it? Of being my brother's keeper? You know what I mean, Savi, when he was alive I doubt we'd met them more than half a dozen times..."

I know, my heart cried out, which is why I can't accept this, this shutting out of me for her.

"And yet the moment I heard of the accident, my heart rushed out to her...and as for Chander...it was as though she became the symbol of the family we've left behind, so irresponsibly shrugged off in our ...you know what I mean.... It was like being back in India...where we are all the time involved in others' problems and joys...not like here where we meet only at parties..."

You are being unfair, I wanted to shout, seeing our ten years of laughter and tears made into so much foam.

Chandri came behind me and put her hand on my shoulder. "I think Chander and I have fallen in love all over again...or maybe for the first time...it is so difficult to say whether the highs we get when newly married is love or just the hungers of the skin.... Now when we come together..."

I didn't understand what she was saying but it came through to me as she went on speaking that in our ten years of sharing she had never divulged anything as personal as what she was telling me now even though I did not half hear her or half understand what I heard.

Savitri:

So we carried it off after all. The temple is still filled with the fragrance of *agarbatti*. I pat myself on the back for keeping the secret so well—I'd told everyone it's a thanksgiving puja for Father's recovery. Because we've been here so long, and word gets around, and the temple is open to all anyway, a lot more people have turned up than we'd expected. Which is fine with us because it is good that we come together in joy, the last time was...and I always cook enough food to feed an army, as Jyoti keeps saying. And friends helped.

The puja was brief and then Sharad took over and announced what the occasion was and you should have heard the cheers. Someone spontaneously started an adaptation of *Jeeyo hazaron saal* and you should have heard the chorus! Then Ajayji, our oldest member, walked up to the podium, totally unplanned of course, and gave a little sermon on marriage. It has been songs and speeches ever since.

* * *

Mohantyji is speaking now; having been a Rotarian back in Bombay, he is holding the floor and the audience, going on and on about Chander's achievements, "as though I am dead" Chander whispers to me.

And now Amar Ghose is singing Rabindra Sangeet. The language of Tagore with its rounded vowels and many sha's and plaintive tune is so soft, so beautiful.

Quite suddenly I feel myself rising above the others. The smell of incense, mingled with the body heat of a hundred and fifty people, is strong up here. Now my head touches the ceiling. Like a helium balloon, I think. I can see everyone, a splash of sari colours and bright summer shirts. How ingenious of Anu to make a salwar suit with her Banarsi silk sari but will the seams hold on so fine a fabric? And there is Pradeep who has dropped out of our crowd after he got married to one of the library clerks. I wonder why they do that? drop us I mean, simply because she is white. To snub us or for fear we'd snub them?

How lovely Chandri is, in her bridal sari of twenty years still shining, and wasn't I clever talking her into wearing it? or did she know what was coming? The actual anniversary is next Wednesday but everything has to be moved to a weekend here, even Diwali.

And there I am, next to Chander, listening to Amar. But I am here too, up here. Seems like everyone we know is here with us. Except Usha, poor Usha, did she guess I was preparing this that she left for Regina to visit a cousin? leaving her children with Chandri?

Children, our children. Suddenly the ceiling is very high and the people below me are very small. The carpet, that has yellow and green geometrical shapes on a red base, is a mere red sweep. Birender Singh's oversize turban is just a blue speck.

I am floating. There are white ants marching from Eaton's towards the Bay. Children! close the doors! I panic. Our children. Why are we here in the temple without them? I notice the curtain has been drawn across the altar, someone must have drawn it after the puja, but they shouldn't have. Open the curtain, we came here to pray for long life...for Chander and Chandri, for all of us, for our children.

It has been great, thanks to Savitri...they are saying. Do they know that I am up here like one of Michaelangelo's cherubs? why didn't he let God's fingers reach Adam's?

The white ants are marching down Pembina Highway, past Drury Manor and into University Crescent. Krish, shut the door, Jai Jyoti where are you? go home quick, the children need you, Krish *beta* be brave you are host to all the little ones, Veejala's and Chandri's and Usha's. Keep them safe. Shut the door.

Termites they call them here. White ants build hills, burrow under house foundations, eat walls. Krish don't open the door, don't talk to strangers, don't die on me, my darling, the white ants are coming.

Far below me Raghavendra is reciting slokas from the Sundara Kanda, nis voice is rich, just right for the sonorous majesty of Sanskrit.

I am not alone any more, my words shrilling across the vacuum. Sharad is by my side. It's all right, love, he's saying, his strong long fingers holding mine. Our children are okay, and theirs too Savi, he says his hand sweeping and covering everyone below, they'll be *okay*, our children will manage okay, they are okay.

We are safe, this is bliss, calm, serene, peaceful. Sharad's hand in mine.

His hold loosens. Don't go, I hold on to him. Don't go, don't. But there is a finger's width between ours. And now the ceiling is higher, so high I can see all of Winnipeg stretched out below me like some wonderland of our dreams, Nehru wrote of Kashmir. Streets neatly laid out, the Assiniboine meandering into the Red, and we shall build our temple at their confluence, we shall bring Ganga to our land our Assiniboine and the fluteplayer, where is the fluteplayer? why have you closed the curtain? especially now, now when the white ants oh god there is another stream of them red and blue and green and they are marching west on Ellice millions of them so we can hardly see the black asphalt of the road or the brown boulevards all seared in the heat of summer.

Dark as kaya blossoms is he, my fluteplayer. Come accept our offering pyare Mohan as you did Sudama's and may all who partake of it ever be in your care pyare Mohan.

Rootless But Green are the Boulevard Trees

Rootless But Green are the Boulevard Trees

Characters

The Bhave family:
    Sharad, the father
    Savitri, the mother
    Jayant, Jyoti, and Krish, their children
Veejala Moghe, Sharad's sister
Anant, Veejala's husband
Vithal and Priti, their children
Arun, Dilip, Rajen, and Sridhar,
    friends of Jayant and Vithal
Andre, Jyoti's boyfriend
Laura, Priti's friend

Winnipeg, March-April, 1979. All scenes take place in the Bhave home in Fort Richmond.

ACT ONE

Scene I

Large built-up basement of a bungalow. The staircase divides the room into two unequal parts. The smaller section is brightly lit; the windows at either end of the room are half piled up with snow, and the light outside them shows it is afternoon. It is about three o'clock.

The sitting area is carpeted with a medium blue "hardtwist" carpet. The play area is tiled. There is a table tennis table half propped up, in the playback position. There are two heavy sponge bats on it and several balls. At the near corner is an open shelf with board games—checkers, Yahtzee, Scrabble, Perquackey, neatly stacked. At the far end is a glass cabinet full of trophies. On the far wall is a dart board, and nine darts in a quill are on the table tennis table. Between the table and the dart board is an open suitcase and a large Adidas sports bag. At the edge of the table are a jogging suit and tennis and squash racquets.

Jayant is putting an album into its flap and walking toward his suitcase from the sitting area. He is nineteen years old, tall for an Indian, soft featured, wavy black hair falling just below his ears; the distinctive feature about him in this scene are his eyes, now smouldering black, angry.

Jyoti, twenty years old, in blue denims similar to Jayant's, is sitting between the suitcase and the dart board on a low ottoman. She is a beautiful girl, in hairstyle and dress typical of her age.

Krish, twelve, comes down the stairs.

KRISH. Hi folks, howdee? Hope you aren't taking the whole collection, Jai.

JAYANT. Jeesus, no, you're welcome to all of it, kid. Got off early?

KRISH. How long will you be gone?

JAYANT. I've told you a dozen times if once, kid, if we can find our way to Europe, we'll be gone a year. If not—(*He shrugs.*)

KRISH. (*Moving from one foot to the other.*) I am going to miss you, Jeesus (*He unconsciously imitates his brother's mannerisms.*), especially on Wednesdays. The papers are so damn heavy. Can you give me a hand today?

JAYANT. Bug off, bozo, you and your paper route.

(*Krish is not quite sure if Jai is being good humoured or angry.*

But when Jayant kicks the Adidas bag clear across the room after looking into it for something, Krish takes the cue and leaves, loudly whistling an Elton John tune to cover his disappointment.)

JYOTI. Krish and dad, especially dad, will miss you.

JAYANT. Let him. Time he knew he is never going to live his dreams through me. Jeesus, just because he was almost, but never, Number One, he's been after me all my life to drive that crummy ball ping ping back and forth.

JYOTI. No one can be so good at anything unless he enjoys doing it. Besides, I've seen your face when you are playing a match, so don't you try to pull that one on me.

JAYANT. Big deal. Provincial champ in a crappy basement game. (*He throws a dart at the board.*)

JYOTI. (*In a cool voice.*) I am glad you are pitching out, and I sure hope it gets into that thick head of yours that we are different, and no matter what we do, we are never going to fit in here. Take to the road, get high, sleep around but still and all.

JAYANT. Fuck off, kid, you'll see.

JYOTI. All these expletives, all the in jargon, but you are never going to be one of the boys. Not that I see why anyone would want to fit into this mould.

JAYANT. Don't *you* come at me with all that crap about morals and Hindu values. I've had an earful from dad nineteen fucking years. He and his pipe dreams about India. Why the hell didn't he stay there? An atomic energy scientist, he was right there from the beginning.... Trombay, planning, the whole bit. He'd have been a director by now. Instead he quits the place to be and rots here selling houses, Jeesus, a crappy real estate broker, just one step better than an encyclopedia salesman....

JYOTI. (*Her face flushed with anger, is about to say something, but instead picks a high-bounce phosphorescent-coloured ball and whams it down on the floor. It bounces between floor and ceiling for the next few minutes as they speak.*) He's not a con man, for God's sake, people need houses (*More assertively.*) and encyclopedias too.

JAYANT. Sure, sure, as much as they need a hole in the head. You know where I got my *Brittanica*? In the Miscellaneous Classifieds I saw this phone number—with the price going down from three hundred to one hundred dollars over three weeks. And then I went there—a shitty little bed-sitter—this young couple. God, nothing in that room cost more than twenty bucks, and here was the five-hundred-dollar *Brittanica* dumped on the sap by a smooth-talking salesman who had played up a sales pitch about self-education in applied electronics. Jeesus. And to think dad has been one of those. (*He picks up a Ping-Pong ball and squeezes it in the palm of his left hand.*)

JYOTI. It couldn't have been easy for him to move out after he was thirty-five, and it is no bed of roses here, mowing the lawn and painting the house and a hundred menial chores which were done by servants in the luxury of family back home.

JAYANT. Some house that, a sprawling shambles handed down untouched from the time of the Peshwas, where you have to walk half a mile to get to the shithouse, Jeesus, we haven't lost anything on that count; even he couldn't think so. And I bet he wouldn't be so maudlin sentimental about that ancestral shack if he were back in Bombay.

JYOTI. And you wouldn't be mouthing vulgarities. Have you ever heard such uncouthness from dad?—ever, ever?

JAYANT. He speaks like out of a book, a mighty bore of a Victorian book, too. Sententious half the time and sentimental the other half.

JYOTI. (*Sarcastically.*) Maybe I spoke too soon, you are halfway to becoming one alright. Equating gentleness with effeminacy, affection with melodrama. (*Musingly, obviously quoting her father.*) To live without tension and yet with dignity, to give our children good food, a liberal education, a healthy environment where, because the body doesn't have to scrounge for sustenance, the spirit can aspire to higher experiences than this sorry world allows.

JAYANT. And the irony is he isn't really sure whether he's given us all these out here. Jeesus, and you know what the trouble is, kid, you are on the moon with that sunshine boy, holding hands and singing moonshine. If you'd get laid a couple of times you'd come off all that preachy repetitions of dad's slogans. Just get laid.

(*He looks at her, and there is something in her eyes that draws him up sharply against the wall of recognition.*)

JAYANT. (*In a low voice.*) You haven't, sis? You haven't. (*It is clear Jyoti has. Jayant is dazed, unwilling to accept it.*)

JAYANT. (*His voice far away.*) Remember that mango tree in Chetan Das's yard back home? And all the raw green mangoes we stole? We never got caught once. And the lichees in Mussoorie that summer. God, they were succulent. And we never got caught then either.

JYOTI. (*Half sarcastically, half gently.*) Good luck, bhau, and

100 *The Door I Shut Behind Me*

when you return to the fold, dad will fix up an upper middle-class, fair-skinned, "homely" Brahmin, as all the matrimonial ads say when they mean "home loving." Virgin, of course.

(*Jayant pulls the darts from the quill and zings them across the room in lightning sequence. All lodge in the inner circle, one dead centre. He picks up his jogging suit and blindly rushes up and out.*)

Scene II

Same day, 4:30 P.M., in the kitchen.

The kitchen is a large rectangular room with a four-by-four-feet china cabinet with glass doors on both sides, which visually divides the dining area from the cooking area. On the top of the china cabinet are (eight-by-ten-inch) framed photographs of each of the children. The dining area is about fifteen feet wide by ten feet deep, while the cooking area is sixteen feet wide and six feet deep. A door, to the left, leads into the hallway to the bedrooms. Another door, to the right, leads to the living room. A door on the upper right leads to the landing and staircase. The dining area has a large window (eight by six feet) through which the sun is shining onto the dining table. In the yard outside are two tall poplars, leafless but shapely, their slender branches waving.

Savitri enters from the back door. She is thirty-nine, light brown, about five feet three inches tall. Her skin is marble smooth, her face comely. She takes off her gloves, places her handbag and a pile of scribblers on a chair, and takes off her boots while leaning against the wall. She takes the boots down the stairs and returns, taking off her coat. She is wearing a pantsuit—black pants, black and grey checked coat, and a silver grey blouse.

Krish enters from the hallway, hockey helmet in hand.

KRISH. Hi, mom!

SAVITRI. (*Walking toward the hallway.*) Rushing off already, beta? Is Jyoti home? Did you have anything to eat or drink? (*She takes an empty A & W mug, which Krish has obviously used, from the table to the sink. She exits, returning a moment later without her coat, jacket, and books.*)

KRISH. Had a large banana milkshake, mom, got rid of all the overripe bananas for you.

SAVITRI. (*Lifting the glass jar from the blender base and rinsing it off at the sink.*) So I see, beta, so I see. (*She wipes the counter top.*)

KRISH. (*Ingratiatingly.*) I'll put the kettle on for you. (*He turns on the stove with the kettle.*)

Rootless But Green 101

SAVITRI. (*Laughing.*) You're a gold brick, beta. Is Jyoti home? (*She washes the teapot in hot water and takes out a teabag from it.*)

KRISH. She was, but if she's still around, she's quiet as a mouse.

SAVITRI. (*Takes her books and bag and walks toward the hallway.*) Don't be late for dinner.

KRISH. No way. Hockey practice at seven. Can I have sixty-five cents mom, for skate sharpening? Just in case I forget later.

SAVITRI. (*Opening her bag.*) Anything else?

KRISH. Hot chocolate?

SAVITRI. (*Handing him a dollar.*) Finished your paper route already?

KRISH. Yeah, we got off at three today.

(*He sits on the steps and ties his boots. Savitri disappears into the hallway and returns, as the kettle whistles, wiping her face, which she has obviously washed. She puts the tea bag in the pot and pours the water. She switches off the stove. She goes out again and when she returns, she has kumkum on her forehead. Krish has meanwhile put on his coat, scarf, and gloves.*)

KRISH. Bye, mom.

SAVITRI. Just check if Jyoti is downstairs, beta.

(*She goes out into the hallway.*)

KRISH. (*After clomping down the stairs and up again.*) Nope, not here. Bye.

(*Savitri comes in, tucking the pleats of her sari at her waist. She looks different now, very brown, very Indian, softly beautiful, and somewhat tired. She pours herself a cup of tea, takes the cup and saucer to the dining table and sits with her back to the window. She props her feet up on another chair. The sun shines on her back. She looks at the photograph of Jyoti on the china cabinet. The photograph shows a beautiful teenager whose eyes, looking just above the camera, are intriguingly sad and whose lips are turned up in a sullen smile.*

Savitri's voice-over expresses her thoughts as she sips her tea and stares at the photograph.)

SAVITRI. (*Voice-over.*) This still core of sadness that veils your eyes, this silence that pales your cheeks, when did you get it, my child, and why?

Conceived in the flood tide of my love, reared in the springtime of my wealth, when did you get it, my child, and why?

In your eyes I hoped to see the flash that brightens mine even now, in your voice I hoped to hear the song of the sky that comes even now to me though never so loud nor often. But you, in the flood tide of first love.... (*She sighs and sits for a moment, a tired look on her face. Then she gets up and energetically sets about getting dinner ready.*)

Scene III

Lights go up on the same scene.

Savitri is stirring something on the stove. Sharad comes in from the living room. He is forty-five, about five feet eight inches tall, and has a smiling face. He is dark complexioned and has a head of black and graying thick straight hair. He has a lean face and a long neck, which he tends to stick out so that his Adam's apple shows even clearer and he looks even taller than he is. Savitri makes him a cup of tea and hands it to him as he seats himself.

SAVITRI. Some biscuits with your tea? Dinner'll be ready in a minute. Was that Jyoti?

SHARAD. No, that was the newsboy. What about Jyoti?

SAVITRI. Oh, nothing. I haven't seen her since yesterday morning, that's all.

SHARAD. You worry too much, Savi. She's alright. Growing to be a beauty, eh? Spit image of you at her age. When I look at the seeds of sadness in her eyes, she looks so much like you. I feel nostalgic and protective and silly. But then I remember how little you needed outside protection. Oh, you were a boarded-up door to those who didn't have a key.

SAVITRI. (*Placing biscuits on the table, she lightly touches Sharad's shoulder and they smile at each other.*) You might like these.

SHARAD. How about a date tonight? Or are you going to be marking papers till two o'clock?

SAVITRI. Not unless you get hooked on the late night movie. (*Sharad pats her on her behind. There is an air of comradeship and being-in-love about them that has little to do with what they say.*)

SAVITRI. I wish Jyoti would come earlier nights.

SHARAD. Don't be a worrier, Savi. She's a good girl, and Andre is a decent boy. He behaves just like one of us. So respectful. And he looks like us too, with his black hair and eyes. Besides, you shouldn't continue to live in the prudish world of our youth. The youngsters here are doing well. They have their own code of morals and they are more idealistic than we give them credit for. This disco craze is perfectly harmless. (*In a tone of explanation as though he knows all about it and she knows nothing.)* A hundred youngsters swaying around; group activities are safety valves that this generation has discovered for itself. As long as they are in a group, they are alright. And thank God for our Winnipeg winters; nobody can wander into the bushes. Least of all *our* children.

(*Savitri smiles sadly as she turns back to the counter. Jayant comes in.*)

JAYANT. (*Squarely placing his hands on his father's shoulder, he helps himself to a biscuit.*) Hi, dad! How was your day? Did Mrs Christopher L. Jones make up her mind, the one who brings marbles to check the level of the floor in each room?

SHARAD. That's Mrs Pringle. Mrs Jones is the one who wants to be a half block away from her church. How's the car?

JAYANT. Guess the old girl is ready for the road but us guys aren't. Now that we are all packed, we are having second thoughts. Jim seems to have discovered he's much more involved with his girl than he'd thought. Dennis doesn't think he has enough bread to have the kind of ball he'd hoped to, out east. I'll have to wait for a weather change in them guys. I noticed your car's been in the garage all day, dad, anything wrong?

SHARAD. Nothing serious. I'd forgotten to plug in the block heater last night. Maybe I should check the battery.

JAYANT. Not on a three-year-old car, dad. But if you wish, I could take it out and have it recharged overnight if necessary. (*He seats himself across from his father.*) Why didn't you wake me up? I could have helped booster from mom's car. You needn't have taken the bus.

SHARAD. (*Shaking his head.*) I should take the bus more often and get used to it, son. It upsets me profoundly to find myself in a crowd. All those alien faces staring at or through you. It makes me wonder. Makes me ask myself, What am I doing here? Who are these faceless people among whom my life is oozing away? Each so self-contained, so complete, looking at me as though I shouldn't be there. It's a strange, eerie feeling, all those discreetly questioning eyes that make me ask endless questions.

SAVITRI. That is why I got myself a car. So I wouldn't have to ask myself questions that perhaps never can be answered. Not to our satisfaction.

SHARAD. How long can we live that way?

JAYANT. (*Good-humouredly.*) To each his own hang-up. When I take a bus downtown, I love it. The Pembina strip is no big deal, an esthetic black hole in fact, but there's something that gets to one's guts even in this barren winter landscape, and suddenly from among the eyesore of billboards and bald trees you see man's indomitable spirit roaring to go up the ski slopes, even if with only a Stanfield brief to hold him up and Cougar boots that centrally heat his soul. Every time the bus goes over the midtown bridge I get a mighty kick thinking of the Indian canoes and the Bay company boats to whom the Red and Assiniboine were once vital lifelines.

SHARAD. (*Who has heartily laughed at Jayant's descriptions.*) You've got something there, Jai, the fascination that rivers and mountains hold. That is why our people raised temples on every hillock and riverbank. Our people....

JAYANT. (*Still good humoured but with an edge of impatience.*) Our people, our old country, dad, there's no "our people" and no "old country" for anyone in the world any more, least of all for us. *This* is our land and here we shall stay.

SHARAD. Roots, son, roots. Can we really grow roots here?

JAYANT. Sure, dad, just look outside. The monstrous new apartment block out there—they have twenty-foot trees around the patio and there are five-footers inside the quadrangle, all set up overnight and flourishing like crazy. If anything, the pollution in the air seems to have acted like pep pills.

SHARAD. That would be a most reassuring analogy, Jai, if our poplar hadn't died. The centre branch didn't bloom last summer, if you remember, and you know what Dave next door said? They are Ontario poplars and not native to Manitoba, and so it is to be expected that they'd dry up one winter, just like that, he said. Looking at them now, who'd think one of them was dead?—that the core is dried up, that the sap isn't flowing up those beautiful branches that form so perfectly shaped a cone? One would think they'd been trimmed every year. If it doesn't bloom this spring, well, we'll have to cut it down. And if an Ontario poplar can't grow and survive in Manitoba soil, what chance do we have?

Scene IV

Same scene as before; the table is set for six but there are only five—Sharad, Savitri, Krish, Jayant, and Priti. Priti—or Pixie, as she is called—is ten years old and resembles Sharad in complexion, hair and eyes. Savitri, sitting at the foot of the table, near the counter, changes dishes, refills, puts them away as they are emptied, generally taking care of the meal and especially serving the younger two. Halfway through the meal, she puts away Jyoti's plate.

PRITI. I have a yukky spoon. I need another one.
SHARAD. A Panchali spoon, eh?
SAVITRI. The dishwasher is acting up again, I think.
JAYANT. Let's call it Panchali. I too need another fork.
PRITI. Tell us the story, uncle, tell us.
KRISH. (*In mock despair.*) Oh, no, not a bedtime tale!
PRITI. Shut up, Krish, close your earflaps.
SHARAD. Haven't you heard it often enough?
PRITI. I like uncle's stories.
SHARAD. One day, when the Pandavas and Panchali were in exile in the forest, Krishna visited them. They had just finished their meal and Panchali had already washed the pots and pans and so....
PRITI. There was nothing left at all for Krishna.
SHARAD. That's right, and he said, "I'm hungry, sister, aren't you going to serve me dinner?" And Panchali thought, "Ohhh! What shall I do?"
KRISH. She didn't even know how to cook.
PRITI. She was a princess, fathead, princesses aren't supposed to cook.
SAVITRI. Do you know from where they got their meal, Krish?
KRISH. Oh, mom! I know the story.
PRITI. Go on, uncle, go on
SHARAD. Well, Krishna said he wanted to see the pot in which Panchali had made the rice.
PRITI. Spinach!
KRISH. Oh, yuk!
SHARAD. Why spinach?
PRITI. Don't you remember we changed it last time from rice to spinach?
KRISH. Doesn't make sense. Cooked rice dries up and sticks to a pot more than spinach.
PRITI. Shut up.
KRISH. You shut up yourself.
SAVITRI. Children, children! Is someone forgetting something?
PRITI. I'm sorry.
JAYANT. Krish?
KRISH. (*With an effort.*) Okay, okay, I'm sorry.
PRITI. Ouch.

JAYANT. (*To Krish in a low voice.*) Quit it, kiddo. (*To Priti.*) Did he kick you?

PRITI. (*Unwilling to reply.*) Let's forget it.

JAYANT. (*Scooping out some ice cream to refill Priti's fruit bowl.*) That's a sport, Pixie, you haven't said anything about school.

PRITI. We have a wall put in our room. The room is so small it's gross.

JAYANT. Be glad you have a wall. The first school I went to had no walls, only a thatched roof.

PRITI. Really?

JAYANT. Yes, really. Granddad started it for the kids on the estate. I was too young to go to regular school and so I'd go there and sit with the kids until lunchtime. Remember, dad, how the roof flew away that second year? And all the baby mangoes fell off the trees?

PRITI. Were you in class?

JAYANT. Nah, I was at St Michael's already. But we didn't have school that day. And panditji quoted some Kabir dohe as we ran toward the cowsheds. He was forever singing Kabir songs.

KRISH. Tell us, Jai, tell us how you used to call him "two-eyes" because he was cockeyed.

PRITI. (*Aggrieved.*) What's that? You've never told me....

JAYANT. We knew his eyes were different from ours but I guess we were stupid or something, eh?

PRITI. Oh, because we *all* have two eyes, right? So what else about him?

KRISH. Jai tells me neat stories. He's a real brother.

PRITI. (*On whom the barb has hit home.*) Vithal doesn't have time, that's why.

KRISH. Betcha don't know about how the toilet in granddad's house didn't have no roof one time for a long time.

PRITI. Really?

JAYANT. And the bakul flowers would fall on us as we did our jobs, oops, sorry, not at the table. (*He makes an exaggerated gesture of apology.*) So, how are your cartwheels, Pixie?

PRITI. Oh, yeah, I forgot to tell you. Your way really works. Thanks, Jai.

JAYANT. Any time, Pix. Here, have half a banana.

PRITI. Do I have to?

JAYANT. A banana a day keeps all problems away. Remember, dad, *my* banana cluster in granddad's house.

Rootless But Green 107

KRISH. (*Aside.*) Whew, why this "remember" binge today?

SHARAD. Pixie, this was a tree we planted on Jai's first birthday and by the time we left, it was a grove.

PRITI. Did you plant one every birthday?

SHARAD. No, not quite, but banana trees have a way of multiplying themselves; there's a saying: "a banana tree always leaves a young tree in its shade."

KRISH. (*In a sing-song voice.*) And every part of the banana tree is useful—its fruit, its leaves as plates, its fibre as string, ta da ta da ta da. (*Jayant is about to reprove Krish but Savitri signals him to desist.*)

JAYANT. Kiddo, I'll have to take you there for you to understand these things. You haven't ever seen a banana tree.

KRISH. There's one in the greenhouse at the Assiniboine Park.

PRITI. Mom said she'd take me to the park last weekend. And the weekend before that. She never did.

SAVITRI. Your mom is a very busy person, Priti.

PRITI. Everyone is busy all the time. Busy, busy, busy.

JAYANT. Almost time for *The Littlest Hobo*. Finish your ice cream quickly, Pixie-Trix.

PRITI. Will you watch with me?

KRISH. Kid stuff.

SAVITRI. Your mom tells me you watch far too much tv.

PRITI. Yeah, but I don't enjoy it unless someone watches it with me.

KRISH. Jai, will you play Othello with me?

JAYANT. (*Patting him on the head.*) You're getting too good for me, kiddo. (*Krish is flattered for a moment but sees himself defeated at getting Jai for himself. His face falls. Jayant notices that but evades direct reversal.*)

JAYANT. But I'll tell you what. I'll take you on if it's Chinese checkers.

KRISH. My way? Jumping over blank holes on each side allowed?

JAYANT. K.O. Your way.

PRITI. But aren't you gonna watch tv with me?

JAYANT. Don't you know me? Napoleon used to dictate four different letters or war plans or whatever to four different people at the same time. Can't you trust me to do two things at once? (*Jayant, Krish, and Priti leave for the living room.*)

SAVITRI. He has a way with children. They're going to miss him. Especially Priti. Poor child.

SHARAD. Fancy him remembering about that thatched roof!

SAVITRI. I've grown used to your nostalgia trips, but this is something new—in Jai. But he's your son, after all. (*She smiles.*)

SHARAD. My son. God bless him.

Scene V

Basement. Same scene as I, except that the Ping-Pong table has been unfolded to the play position. Jayant's bags, etc. are now under the table. Jayant is kneeling on the floor, transferring the last of the contents from a suitcase to the floor. As he speaks, he puts them one by one into a slightly larger suitcase. Vithal comes in. He is two years older than Jayant but looks more of a man. Feature for feature, he resembles his cousin but the resemblance is obscured by the difference in their personalities. Vithal is an angry young man, though his face transforms into that of a pleasant youngster when he smiles. He has a moustache, and the attractive hirsuteness of one whose beard grows fast. Jayant's face lights up on seeing Vithal. Though Jayant is a couple of inches taller, it seems that whenever they look at each other Jayant is looking up and Vithal down.

VITHAL. (*Holding a car compass.*) I almost forgot to give you this. It is still functional, but I'd suggest you buy another more reliable one. Worth the few extra bucks, I can tell you. Those roads in the Laurentians could be one hell of a maze once you get off the highway. By the way, I did tell you about the quirks of the luggage rack, right?

JAYANT. Instead of all these directions and instructions, why don't you join us, Vith? Come along. (*He gets excited as he speaks.*) Come on Vith, I've been wanting to ask you all along. Wow, we'd have a ball. Please. We could leave the rest of the gang in Montreal; they want to hang out there for a while, a coupla weeks with Don, Don Blackwood, remember him? We can take off on that canoe trip you've always wanted. Montmorenci.... Come on, Vithal. This is the time. (*Vithal says nothing. He continues to bounce a ball low on the table, bringing the bat slowly down. The sound of the drawn-out crunch provides a background song.*) I've had some great times, Vith, but the greatest have been with you, when it was just us two. Jeez, the things you've taught me! I was one raw hunk of a kid in '72. Didn't know even how to tie a slipknot. But the things I knew by the time we returned! And then our summer in India (*He whistles.*). I thought we were packed off there for granddad's sixtieth birthday just to please the folks back home, and I hated leaving Winnipeg. But Jeez, that was the best time I've ever had. We were a great team, remember the time in Delhi we lost our way near Sikander Tomb and…. Oh, Vithal, please do come. Say the word and I'll drop out of the gang. Who needs them anyhow? But we have to get out of this asshole. We are just killing ourselves here. Parents are such a pain in the ass, let's go. I can't stand them.

VITHAL. (*With startling vehemence*.) Quit talkin', fella, running away, that's all everyone thinks of, run away, tuck your tail between your legs and scram the moment some problem comes up. But you, you want someone to hang on to even when running away. You've done nothing but hang on to apron strings all your life. And all the time ranting all that bullshit about growing up and being on your own. You are just one hell of a mixed-up bounder. Deep inside, all you want is to suck your thumb and dream of granddad's estate. You're pissed off, Jayant; you and your hang-ups; resenting your dad because he is in some humdrum business and not a superscientist; and yet you are emotionally tied to his coattail; one harsh word from him and you are ready to snivel like a sissy schoolgirl.

Oh, man, isn't it time you were to someone what he's been to you? What I've been to you? What every goddam person around you has been to you? Instead of being an obnoxious leech with a thumbsucking ego?

All you can think of is running away. Run away, like a coward. God, I'm sick of you, sick of the whole lot of runners away. (*Vithal's onslaught has annihilated Jayant. He sits there, looking up with pained bafflement, a dog that has been suddenly kicked by his master. He gets up slowly from his crouched stance on the floor, slowly collects Ping-Pong balls from the floor and sofas, and mechanically drops each with trembling fingers into a Halex carton. The chore composes him somewhat, but he still has a dazed expression. Vithal, meanwhile, is leaning his elbow against the near wall, bat in hand, holding his head.*)

VITHAL. (*In a subdued way.*) I am sorry, Jay, taking it out on you like that. I…I have problems. I'm sorry.

JAYANT. (*Eagerly accepting the apology.*) We are all made that way, I guess, a family of volcanoes, except for Jyoti. I wish…do you know that Jyo…. Let's play. (*Takes up a bat.*)

VITHAL. (*Without moving.*) Mom is leaving us.

JAYANT. (*Shocked.*) No! She can't do that. (*Whispers.*) That's all over long ago.... She can't do that! (*His voice breaking*.) What are we going to do? Jeesus, what we gonna do?

VITHAL. (*Comes to the table and takes out a ball from the carton*.) I think I've found a way to return that double spin of yours. Here. Rally.

Scene VI

The next day, lunch hour.

Savitri comes down the basement steps, calling "Jyoti!" The hi-fi is on full volume. The sitting area lights up. Jyoti is on the couch, her feet on an ottoman. There are textbooks all around. She reaches out and turns down the volume on the hi-fi. Savitri comes in. She is in her school outfit, with a cardigan instead of a jacket. By habit, as she talks she puts things back in place—magazines off the television top into the magazine rack, socks off the floor, etc.

SAVITRI. (*Without looking at Jyoti after the first glance*.) I don't want you to use your father's car in the evening from now on. Any time you need a car, take mine, and if I have to go out again after work, *I* shall take dad's car. Is that clear?

JYOTI. What's the big deal? There isn't a scratch on the Chrysler, not from me. So what's the to-do?

SAVITRI. Because.

JYOTI. We outgrew that reason ten years ago, mother.

SAVITRI. (*With sudden vehemence*.) Yes, we are supposed to treat you as rational adults even when you behave like beasts. (*She takes out an open condom pack from her cardigan pocket and flings it against the back of the recliner*.) I don't know whether you want to prove something to me or whether you meant to flaunt this to your father or what, but I don't want this to happen in dad's car, ever.

JYOTI. Big deal, mom, it was just an accident that it dropped out. I didn't even know. And who needs a car for that, anyway. As for dad, what makes you think he'll flip his lid any more than you? You help him on with his blinkers night and day, you trot him out and into his ivory tower all the time, but surely no one could have lived here ten years without....

SAVITRI. How long has this been going on?

JYOTI. (*Mockingly*.) I don't think you'd like the answer to that.

SAVITRI. (*Taken aback, she pulls herself together with an effort*.) I'll take you to Doctor MacRae and put you on the pill. (*She shrugs*.) Maybe I'm out of date there too, maybe a mother is not *needed anymore even for that. (With firmness.)* But you *will* go to him, Jyoti. *(Then she adds after a pause.)* If you haven't already, of course.

JYOTI. *(Picks up the pack and sticks it into her handbag.)* Ramses! Damn romantic name for a goddam rubber.

SAVITRI. *(Startled by the bitterness in the girl's voice, she moves forward.)* Jyoti.... *(Jyoti turns away.)*

SAVITRI. *(Mockingly.)* If that's how blase you are about it, I pity you, Jyoti, I pity you.

JYOTI. *(Collecting several of her books, speaks with studied casualness.)* I'd better run before you get behind your lectern. *(She leaves.)*

SAVITRI. *(Her hands on the back of the recliner, she stands still while the voice-over comes on.)* Ramses. When you said that, my darling, I wanted to hold you to myself, lick away your tears, smooth away your fears, take you back into myself and wrap you and keep you. Instead I spoke to you as to a woman, someone not myself, a woman I wanted to hurt and claw.

ACT TWO

Scene I

Saturday morning, about 11:00 A.M.

Jyoti is having breakfast in the kitchen. She is in blue jeans and a loose, open-collared shirt. The doorbell rings. Jyoti goes toward the living room. Sound of door opening and Jyoti effusively greeting someone. Sridhar and Jyoti enter kitchen. In looks and speech, Sridhar is different from the other young men. The lilt in his accent and his vocabulary show he has been educated in India's public schools. He is darker than the others and has a hairline that recedes at the left. He is not good-looking but has an intellectual and sensitive face that makes him stand out in any company.

SRIDHAR. Why the welcome mat? Something wrong? Did Krish beat you at Othello? Andre not turn up? Mom refuse you the car? Prof. make mincemeat of your term paper?

JYOTI. (*Laughing.*) A little of everything. But mainly it is Saturday morning. That's why. Do I look that beaten up? How did you know I was feeling driven up the wall?

SRIDHAR. Been sitting three years on your doorstep, remember? Where's everyone?

JYOTI. Mom and dad have gone shopping.

SRIDHAR. Dad shopping?

JYOTI. A haircut maybe, while mom shops. I dunno. Krish must be somewhere in the bay. And Jayant's under the car as usual, I suppose, at Jim's.

SRIDHAR. Some host. Invites me for lunch and disappears.

JYOTI. For lunch? Are you sure?

SRIDHAR. Of course I am sure. Not just me. The whole gang, he said, since this might be his last weekend.

JYOTI. Lunch, eh? (*Gets up and starts clearing the table.*) I'd better get something started. Mom's expecting you all for dinner. (*Opens oven.*) Yes, there's mattar paneer all made. But nothing else. Might as well put the boiler on for a quick pilao. (*Takes out rice boiler, fills it with water and measures out rice as they talk.*)

SRIDHAR. Have they decided just when they are hitting the road?

JYOTI. Haven't a clue. As soon as they can get the jalopy in shape, I guess. It is spring everywhere else. (*She turns toward Sridhar.*) Have you taken a look at it, Shri? Is it really safe? It didn't look anything like a car when they brought it in first.

SRIDHAR. They know what they are doing. Jim has fixed up a neat ramp at his own place. They are pros.

JYOTI. But you are in mechanical engineering, and you've been right into car building. You'd know better.

SRIDHAR. No one's asked me and I am not a guy that butts in.

JYOTI. Why so formal?

SRIDHAR. Mine's only book knowledge. Jim and Dennis have worked in garages summers since they were aye high.

JYOTI. (*With a quick glance at him.*) Is that what they say or how you feel?

SRIDHAR. (*With a sheepish smile.*) A little of both, I guess. Just one of those hang-ups we grad students have when we come up against real-life mechanics.

JYOTI. Shri, I'd feel happier if you would check the car. They don't even have the right tools, just some primitive throwaways. Please.

SRIDHAR. (*Bowing.*) Anything you say, ma'am. Any time, ma'am. (*They laugh.*)

JYOTI. You're a sport. I feel so comfy with you. (*She takes a cauliflower out of the refrigerator and cuts it as they talk.*)

SRIDHAR. I should feel flattered. If I didn't know something was up. What is it? Here's a shoulder to cry on.

JYOTI. I'll take a raincheck on that, because things aren't all that bad yet. Everyone's a bit nervy with Jayant all set to go, that's all. It is nice to have someone to talk to, someone to growl at, someone to laugh with, someone who knows all about the family. As a matter of fact, everything is dandy! It is great to be alive and in love.

SRIDHAR. With Andre. And me rooted to your doorstep three years. (*He throws up his hands in mock despair.*)

JYOTI. Oh, be serious.

SRIDHAR. Okay, okay. (*He literally wipes a grin off his face.*) What's your problem?

JYOTI. It is not a problem. Everything is so extreme—so ecstatic and so depressing, so high and so low. And I am so inarticulate. He used to think I was cold blooded because I never let on.

SRIDHAR. (*Stiffens momentarily and then shrugs exaggeratedly.*) Never let on about clammy hands and shortwindedness, tingle and all, right? But you can talk to me about it, right? Third-person syndrome, right? (*Jyoti does not say anything but the colour rises on her cheeks.*) And your slide projector inside keeps shooting a million angles of the same face, right?

JYOTI. (*Changing the subject.*) Will you be going to Detroit with that electric car for the show?

SRIDHAR. Does he feel that way? Does he really, really feel that way? That's the nagging question, right?

JYOTI. (*Provoked.*) Of course he does. Every fibre in your being can't quiver unless the vibes are mutual.

SRIDHAR. (*Passionately.*) Can't it, God, can't it? (*Recovering his usual flamboyance.*) Every nerve, every hair erect, and not just hair, I can tell you.

JYOTI. (*With biting coolness.*) That sounds like a wisecrack you've been rehearsing "to tell the boys."

SRIDHAR. (*Stung to the quick, he flares up.*) Damn you, I must be mad to come here. God, how I wish I could hate and have done with you. Time was all of Winnipeg was brighter because of you, every day a gateway to Eden and I would go to sleep touching the tips of your fingers. But now I can't get to sleep until I have exhausted myself ripping you up, until I rape and rip you apart night after night. Damn you and damn that s.o.b. Adonis of yours. (*He walks out of the room. Sound of front doors slamming shut. Jyoti continues to cut the cauliflower, her face hidden by her hair.*)

Scene II

Lights up again on the same scene but with Jyoti placing a lid on a skillet on the stove. Sound of back door being opened. Sound of boots being scraped, and of voices. Jayant enters first, and as he speaks, others enter one by one—Arun, Vithal, Rajen, and Dilip.

JAYANT. Hi mom! Mom? Oh, hi, Jyoti, something smells good. What a sport. Thanks, Jyo, I meant to phone mom we were coming for lunch, not dinner, but before I knew it, wham, it was lunch time. Was that Shri whipping out of the bay at a hundred miles an hour? He told you about lunch, I suppose. Did you send him out to buy something?

Come on you guys. Looks like we're going to get lunch sooner than I thought, but we'd better have something anyway. How about mango sundae?

(*He takes out a can of mango pulp and fixes up the blender with milk and vanilla ice cream. The others, meanwhile, have greeted Jyoti, all except Dilip. Jayant draws up a chair for Dilip and introduces him.*)

Sorry for not doing the honours properly—Jyoti this is Dilip;

he's just come from IIT Delhi this term. And this is my sis. Sit down fellows. (*He goes back to his milkshake making.*)

VITHAL. Let me help with something. What's cooking?

JYOTI. (*Pleased to see him.*) That's anybody's guess. Mom's made enough mattar paneer to feed an army and pilao will be ready as soon as the vegetables are done. Any suggestions?

VITHAL. How about puris? I haven't had a good Indian meal in ages. Here, I'll get the dough ready. Arun, it is time you washed your eyes; slice some onions for raita.

(*He is obviously familiar with the kitchen, and in a trice has mixing bowl, flour, etc. on the table. Sound of back door opening. Sridhar enters.*)

JAYANT. Come on in, Shri, the way you vroomed away I thought you were out to kill.

SRIDHAR. (*His usual self now.*) Me kill? Gentle as a baa lamb. If anything, I am just a wet doormat for people to walk over. (*He sits down. Jyoti and he do not look at each other directly at any time. He takes out a scratch pad and doodles and draws through the scene.*)

VITHAL. Arun, what were you moaning about this evening?

ARUN. (*Taking onion and knife.*) Yeah, I can't make it. I have to be at the International Students' at eight.

JAYANT. That crappy joint? How can you stand it?

ARUN. I am stuck with it for the year. Thank God it is almost over.

RAJEN. Any nice girls, yaar?

JAYANT. You kidding? You know the type. A cross between do-gooders and husband hunters.

ARUN. Come on, be fair.

JAYANT. Okay, I'll be fair. I haven't met anyone there with a semblance of good looks or intelligence but many with hearts of gold.

RAJEN. Met the other kind anywhere?

JAYANT. You have a point, man, they don't come in that brand any more.

RAJEN. They must be somewhere. Drat it. When I first came, everyone knew everyone else, but now there are such droves of them you don't get to know anyone. We can't seem to find any smart girls. Present company excepted, of course.

JYOTI. Thanks.

RAJEN. Tell me, Jyoti, what's the matter with girls, Indian girls, I mean. One tries to say a friendly hello and they freeze up like we were making a pass.

ARUN. What gets my goat is the way they all honeymunch with others. It shames the pants off us to see our girls smiling sweety sweet with everyone but us. They need to get their noses punched.

RAJEN. Sure, go ahead, if you can reach above their belly buttons, that is. Or do you mean to punch the girls' noses?

ARUN. Three girls, yessiree three got hitched up this year. And I could name a dozen who are going steady or going out anyway.

JYOTI. There are three hundred who didn't.

ARUN. Them. They are so conservative they'd wear purdah if their dads told them to.

DILIP. (*In an aside to Sridhar.*) The other day I was at the Shahs' and there were quite a few young people. It reminded me of back home.

ARUN. Three girls! Not one, not two, girls are such dum dums.

RAJEN. Present company excepted, of course.

VITHAL. No need to except it, dammit. Tell us Jyoti, man to man, why this rash of dating whites? And don't come up with the usual nonsense about love at first sight.

RAJEN. And keep off the double standards bit as well. We guys have to mumbo jumbo white girls only because our own girls are such touch-me-nots.

JYOTI. What can I say? You've forbidden both logical answers there are.

VITHAL. Logic, my ass. Love at first sight is baloney. One falls in love for the qualities one sees.

JYOTI. A dozen people around may have those qualities, but you happen to fall for a particular one. It just happens.

SRIDHAR. Vibes, man, vibes. (*He gesticulates with his fingers.*) Supersensory antennae zoom like a jack-in-the-box the moment Prince Charming appears.

RAJEN. Or Princess Charming. Let's not be sexist.

ARUN. But aren't we off the track? Who's talking about love and marriage? Just sitting together over a pizza, a movie maybe.

RAJEN. Oh, that? No squeezing hands and maybe hmm. (*Several laugh.*)

JAYANT. (*In a cool voice but with undertone of vehemence.*) That's the problem, you guys are so naive, the most you can think of is squeezing hands. Maybe if you offered to screw them you'd have them at your feet.

ARUN. Easy, easy, there's a limit to jokes in mixed company.

VITHAL. Jyoti's okay. She's one of us. You still haven't answered, though.

JYOTI. Oh, I didn't think you wanted an answer. You are all like the six blind men and the elephant, each talking about a different thing altogether. And liking the sound of your own voice, no matter what the other guys say. But that is alright, because there are as many types of dating as you can think of and girls for every type, if you'd just stop talking and do something. Ask Dilip about the three hundred girls you've rejected out of hand now. You guys notice only the few who do something a bit off the beaten path.

RAJEN. (*Aside.*) A Freudian slip that?

JYOTI. As for dating local style, we have to change with time. Haven't we been in the closet long enough? I don't mean just girls. All of us.

JAYANT. (*Half mockingly.*) Say, that's profound, ain't it? We have to change. Sounds so good when you say it, and yet you know what? Just the other day someone said just the opposite and it sounded even better. "Take to the road, get stoned, sleep around but you'll never become one of them. Why anyone would want to become one of them beats me," those were the words.

DILIP. (*Somewhat hesitantly, feeling a newcomer in a closed group and yet eager to speak.*) But, it seems to me, you should make every effort to merge since you are here to stay. I mean, this is your country, the only land you know and will know. You have to try to assimilate, don't you think? The whites would appreciate that effort.

VITHAL. Assimilate, my ass. They don't want us to assimilate. They want us out. We'll be squashed like bugs soon. All these years we thought the isolation was coming from us, but now that we are trying to merge we know exactly what they feel. They've never wanted us and now we are a threat. Serves us right for wanting to try to be one of them. We have to stay separate from them and stay together within and we've got to show them that we have as much right to be here as the pissed-off whites who've bullied their way into this country these last three hundred years. We've got to stay apart, stay together. That's the only way.

DILIP. (*Impressed but still puzzled.*) But what's the point of living in ghettoes?

RAJEN. Good word, yaar. But that's called multiculturalism out here. Each group stays together and once a year there's a three-ring circus, a zoo called Folkorama where everyone visits everyone else's cage. Hula, Calypso, bagpipes and all. Just wait for the mela. I'll take you around. Except that everyone gets drunk after about ten every night.

VITHAL. (*Continuing as though Rajen hadn't spoken.*) Ghettoes is right. But we need ghettoes. Look at the Jews. They've been ghettoed for centuries and they've chosen to ghetto themselves even if they didn't have to. Only in ghettoes can unity thrive. They toughened themselves, did everything five times better than the others and now they don't get pushed around any more. They are top of the world.

RAJEN. Now that they are the tops, now that they are accepted and all that, do you see the writing on the wall? They are disintegrating, just melting into the sea of society. They are dying, in short. What an anticlimax. Tst. Tst. No more Einsteins, or even Philip Roths. They'll be finished. Schlemiel, schlimazel, shlep, kvetch, all gone; knish, blintz, borscht, all gone. Oi vey!

VITHAL. Don't fool around, man. We've got to stand tall. And by God we shall. We shall build our temple at the confluence of the Red and Assiniboine and then we shall say Okay, we are ready to assimilate. Not here not now. Now it'll be bootlicking, applepolishing.

ARUN. Come on, Vith old man, I thought you'd have grown out of the Naxalite phase by now.

VITHAL. Go ahead, be patronizing. But if your house gets stones and eggs smashed on the window, you'll get action faster from them than from any goddam cop. That's the writing on the wall, that we can't expect nothing from these pissed-off bastards. Living like goddam ostriches, that's what we are.

ARUN. How are your Desh Hall friends? Haven't seen them around campus for quite a while.

VITHAL. (*Suddenly quiet.*) I don't go there any more. (*Everyone falls silent, infected by Vithal's sudden depression. Realizing that, Vithal rallies.*)

VITHAL. I have personal problems, boys. I am too busy making it to hell on my own to bother about missionary zealots.

ARUN. Anything we can do to help?

RAJEN. We'll sock it to her. Gently but firmly. Just tell us who. With a Don Juan like you, we wouldn't want to bonk the wrong one.

VITHAL. I'll do it myself. Thanks anyway. More milkshake there?

JAYANT. (*Passing the milkshake.*) Vithal, you sound good, man, but your arguments are a washout. Why should we fall on the neck of bastards who'd be way out of our orbit in India? One makes one's friends for their qualities, as you yourself said, not for their skin colour. Face it, man, we don't have anything in common with the other half of the Indians here. Why the hell do we have to rub shoulders with them simply because we happen to come from the same political entity? That's all India is, a political entity that came together as a nation after a zillion years because the British made it so.

VITHAL. British, my ass.

JAYANT. Cool it, man, I know my history as well as you. Asoka, Akbar, Aurangzeb—all ruled all of India but they didn't have a nation, not by a long shot.

RAJEN. Don't forget Sivaji, Jai Bhavani, Har Har Mahadev ki Jai.

JAYANT. (*Lightly giving him an uppercut on his right jaw.*) No one makes fun of Sivaji under this roof. But no one.

RAJEN. (*Gamely.*) How about Ram Rajya?

DILIP. (*Leaning forward excitedly.*) You can't use that flippant tone for Ram Rajya. It has held us together from within. Rama, Krishna, Govinda—that's the essential truth, and because of that we've been a nation for five thousand years!

JAYANT. Right ho, sir, but let's come to *us*. Why in sacred hell, give me one solid reason in hell, why we should paw around with illiterates who troop into airports carrying kerosene tins and bedding rolls. I've seen them, Jeesus, mucking up all of Heathrow with stinking masalas and turbans. And (*He turns to Vithal.*) I have news for you and your favourite story about the *Komagata Maru*. I'll come to that in a sec. (*He continues to speak and gesticulate but his voice is not heard while Rajen is heard in an aside to Dilip.*)

RAJEN. (*Aside to Dilip.*) This was a ship chartered by a Sardarji back in 1914 to circumvent the immigration regulation that said colonials immigrating into Canada had to come straight from a British colony direct into Canada. It was Canadian Immigration's sneaky way of preventing brown immigrants, since there was no direct service between Canada and the Far East. This ship—*Komagata Maru*—was quarantined and starved off Vancouver for a month and then the passengers were shunted back to India, a shameful, ignominious episode for everyone concerned.

JAYANT. That guy who chartered it—Gurdip Singh—was a cheapskate two-bit crook who was leading four hundred suckers who thought they could get rich quick. Skidrow bums led by a scoundrel. I read a book about it.

RAJEN. Really? Where'd you get it, yaar?

VITHAL. I know the book. Written by a white, what else could you expect?

RAJEN. Sure, sure. Whites would whitewash the white bar-

barism, and a brown writer would tan the whites. What the saga needs is an impartial outsider, a Chinese. But you never can tell. Yellow is nearer to white than brown. Tst, tst.

JAYANT. Quit kidding, Jeesus, these scum bums.

ARUN. Easy, easy, forget your lord-of-the-manor past, Jay, this is a classless society.

VITHAL. Shows how little you know about this society. But hang classlessness, and what have you. It's a plain question of survival. If we don't stand together, we don't have a chance.

JAYANT. Count me out. They've brought nothing but a bad name on us. Getting convicted for rape and murder.

ARUN. Easy, easy, when there are a hundred thousand people, there's bound to be a coupla crooks and maniacs among them.

VITHAL. I agree, you guys, but do you read the story between the lines, the editorial slant of how quick they are to identify the colour and country of the few who get into trouble? Exploiters and sensationalists.

JAYANT. Why don't you talk about the exploiting slave drivers out west? That show last Saturday just about killed me.

VITHAL. What show?

RAJEN. It was a documentary on farmhelpers in B.C.

JAYANT. We were at Larry's watching the game. I had the remote control, and commercial time I switched channels, and there it was—poor illiterate Panjabis bundled off into unheated shacks. And who was their employer? A son of a gun Panjabi. I was so paralyzed with shame I couldn't press the damned button to change channels. Jim was decent enough to pass it off with a "C'mon you guys, get back to the game."

VITHAL. You have a decent lot of friends. I'll hand that to you and to them. Real decent guys, and I'd be proud of you if your head wasn't screwed the wrong way.

RAJEN. Hey, Shri, you haven't said a word. Open up, yaar, let's have your words of wisdom.

SRIDHAR. (*Who has been doodling intricate border designs on his pad.*) I think I know what Vithal's getting at. Jay gets so het up because he identifies himself emotionally with every brown face he sees. Vithal, on the other hand, is far more detached despite his fanaticism. He's calling for political identification, or coalition rather.

RAJEN. Hear hear, Mr Speaker.

SRIDHAR. Okay, I know I sound like a pretentious sociologist, but I mean, hell, why does it have to be "them" and "us" all the time, why not just you and me, an individualistic approach; the best bet is to let time take its course, and come a couple of generations everything would be more even all around, within the community and outside; we'd have a lot more brown-white kids and the problems....

RAJEN. As Mrs Rabbit said to Mr Rabbit when they were chased by the hunting dogs—hang on a while longer and we'll outnumber....

ARUN. You know what you sound like, Shri? (*He lifts his hand in a Nazi salute.*) Heil Hitler! Heil Idi Amin! Forced marriages for a new improved race.

RAJEN. And Heil Margaret Thatcher, though she doesn't know it is the same thing.

VITHAL. People get what they deserve. And our history shows just what we deserve. Tyrants and traitors. Bin Tughlak, Sirajuddin Dowla, Jalianwala Bagh.

ARUN. And our liege lady who is staging a comeback.

RAJEN. Tyrants, traitors, and? You need another category for Sterling Lyon and Joe Clark. (*Everyone laughs except Vithal.*)

VITHAL. (*Suddenly more violently explosive than ever before.*) Goddamned ostriches and cowards. Utterly selfish, that's what we are. Damn, double damn. (*He punches the dough.*)

(*Sound of the back door opening. Savitri comes in, grocery bags in both arms. The boys take the bags from her. Rajen slips into his boots and goes out. Arun is about to follow but Savitri stops him.*)

SAVITRI. Don't go. There are only two more bags. (*She goes down to the landing and comes back without her boots and with coat in hand.*) Hullo, boys. I am glad to see you. I do hope you won't forget us altogether once Jayant leaves. How is your mother's arm, Arun? Thank you, Rajen. (*Rajen says something.*) Yes, I know, he told me he'd be back in half an hour. Here, let me take over. Down you go, boys, and come up again in half an hour. Don't start any long-drawn game or debate. Lunch will be ready soon.

RAJEN. Take your time, Mrs Bhave, we're stuffed for the nonce. With Jay's milkshake and Vithal's speeches. (*All the boys, except Vithal, go down. Vithal continues to knead the dough.*)

SAVITRI. Jyoti, thanks for starting the lunch. I thought they were coming for dinner!

JYOTI. You know Jayant, mom.

SAVITRI. It's wonderful to have a houseful of voices. I do hope they continue to drop in.

Scene III

Same scene as before.

SAVITRI. (*Goes to Vithal and touches his arm.*) How are you, beta? You haven't been here since a long time. You are coming to the university everyday, aren't you? (*She waits expectantly but Vithal only smiles at the dough.*) You haven't dropped any courses, have you?

VITHAL. (*Looks up and smiles pleasantly.*) No, but only because I'd forgotten about the deadline for voluntary withdrawals.

SAVITRI. Beta, finish that degree. Just a few weeks of work and it will be over.

VITHAL. Does it matter?

SAVITRI. The degree itself doesn't. But completing something you've started does. Let's make a deal. You write the exams, and I'll....

VITHAL. Exams and courses aren't the problem, kaku.

SAVITRI. Donna? How's Donna?

VITHAL. (*Distantly.*) Oh, that's been off a long time.

SAVITRI. Something that's been on for five years can't be turned off that easily.

VITHAL. It wasn't easy.

SAVITRI. I can't believe Donna would break it off. I know her. She's devoted to you.

VITHAL. *She* didn't.

SAVITRI. Beta! You? Why would you do that? Donna is one in a million.

VITHAL. (*Bitterly.*) But I'm a dime a dozen. A habitual dropout, a drag. And she is halfway to being a doctor.

SAVITRI. Stop belittling yourself. You have the Midas touch, Vithal, but you refuse to touch anything. Any and every thing you do would be done superlatively well but you drop it without ever trying. Maybe you aren't into the university program. Get back to RRCC and finish one of the courses you started last year.

VITHAL. And become a cruddy electrician? Or would you rather I finish the masonry course? Or the plumbing?

SAVITRI. It would make no difference to us. And it would make no difference to Donna. I know her.

VITHAL. I believe it, kaku. You'll love me as much, but you'd still wish I'd chosen to touch something else with my Midas touch.

Donna too. She'll love me, sure, and so would any children we might have, so would they all, all honourable men. But I have neither wit nor words.... Deep down, way down she would have that core of disappointment. A basic imbalance.... A professional woman has certain fundamental standards, expectations.

SAVITRI. You are being unfair to her. In personal relationships that one makes with open eyes, one....

VITHAL. We'll start off with the best of intentions, don't doubt that. But she will go on, zooming ahead, and just give up on me after a while.

SAVITRI. Donna is more Hindu than many of us.

VITHAL. I don't doubt it. She'd never divorce me, indeed, we'd be a great couple from the outside, especially if I kept away from a full-time profession. But the core, at the core something would be missing. A woman, even a Hindu-like woman, maybe especially a Hindu-like woman, expects her man to be up there, higher than herself, and woe to the man who can't be a demigod. All the other men they will sympathize with, and even admire, but their own man? Oh, no, he has to be some kind of a titan. Ain't I right? Ain't I?

SAVITRI. Get up there, Vithal, you can climb to the top of any ladder you want. Why don't you do something new? Join politics. It is time we had some of our people there. Your Desh Hall friends, isn't that what they say?

VITHAL. I don't go there any more. (*Again his voice is dispirited, but this time he does not rally from the silence that follows. Then he speaks slowly.*) You can do all these controversial, way out things only when you are basically happy. If I get into a violent situation now, and that comes naturally at the Desh Hall, even if it were exactly what I've been doing forever, everyone would promptly trace it to a broken home or a broken affair or whatever. (*In silence Jyoti and Savitri continue to move about from counter to table to refrigerator.*)

SAVITRI. Veejala was to have lunch with me at school yesterday but didn't turn up. Last Monday she phoned and postponed the lunch to yesterday, but this time she didn't even phone.

VITHAL. (*Getting up.*) She needs you. (*More softly.*) I guess we all do. (*He goes down.*)

JYOTI. (*Slowly, fearfully.*) Is something the matter?

SAVITRI. He's always been a moody boy, how was he before I came?

JYOTI. (*More relaxed.*) His usual self, I thought. Talking nonstop. With more gusto, if anything, because he had a captive audience in this boy who's just come from Delhi. The usual high; *you* know Vithal, about "we have the same rights as these pissed-off whites, we'll build a temple on the Red and Assiniboine," and all that stuff we've heard a hundred times.

SAVITRI. (*Quietly.*) Yet every time I hear him, I am moved by those words. Even though I don't feel the same way. Some day, I hope, Vithal and all of you will realize that we have already built that temple because we carry our gods within us and with us wherever we go.

JYOTI. (*Fearful again.*) What did he say about auntie? What did he mean? Tell me, mom, what's happening?

SAVITRI. (*Reassuringly calm.*) Veejala has always been a rebel. I don't think I've told you of the pandemonium she created soon after my wedding. I came to know later that it was only one of many, but it was a storm such as I'd never known in my father's house. She sold her diamond ring so she could enrol in an aviation course; the family had said no, and so she went right ahead and got the money anyway. The ring was a family heirloom, given by Peshwa Balaji Rao, and you can imagine the furor. She has done some wonderfully crazy things, as you know.

JYOTI. (*Admiringly.*) She's neat. Always on the go, stunning every which way, looks, confidence.

SAVITRI. She makes it so very difficult for one to excuse her actions, but I have always found it even more difficult not to.

JYOTI. She's a sloppy housewife, though. Poor Vithal, I am sure, hasn't had a good meal in ages. All the puris and raita were his idea.

SAVITRI. Vee was never much of a housewife. Back home she was used to returning from work and finding a hot dinner ready, clothes washed, the house spic and span; it hasn't been easy to adjust.

JYOTI. (*Stung into a kind of jealousy.*) But she's been here a lot longer than you and—

SAVITRI. (*In a reminiscing voice.*) That flat they had in Delhi when they returned from the States. Fabulous gadgets we had seen only in pictures. Electric range, toaster, oven, washing machine... and a fleet of servants too.

JYOTI. Oh, mom, beat it, she has hired help here too. If anything, you are the one who's got a bad deal. Granddad's house, wow, what a mansion, and here you are working your fingers to the bone, scrubbing and polishing (*With sudden passion.*). I'll start hating this place the day your hands lose their softness.

SAVITRI. They'll survive, beti, they'll survive, but will our spirits? No matter how long we live here, it is never long enough to forget either our old ways or our old comforts.

JYOTI. (*Laughing indulgently.*) Mom, you've just finished saying we carry our temple within us, and now this. There's consistency for you.

SAVITRI. (*Laughing.*) Is that inconsistent? You youngsters corner us at every turn. I don't know, Jyotishma, I used to believe that if only I could take time out from housework and school to think, I could sort out all the questions, iron out all the inconsistencies and find out what life is all about. But I have never really tried to make time. I suppose I am afraid of the answers. What if there's no pot of gold at the end of the rainbow? So we take up more chores than we can handle and we make sure we never have leisure enough to think. It works well most of the time but those few times we *are* faced with some brutal truth, we panic, we just can't cope, and we lash out at each other.

(*She looks at Jyoti, who looks back. They stand a moment, their eyes locked in understanding and compassion, and they simultaneously get back to work.*)

Scene IV

Afternoon, Savitri is drinking tea as in Scene III of Act One. Sharad enters, his face flushed and upset. He comes in and thuds onto a chair. He takes off his gloves but not his parka. His boots make a slow puddle at his feet as the scene progresses.

SHARAD. What is this about Veejal? Why didn't you tell me all these days?

SAVITRI. What did she say? Would you like some tea? (*She moves as though to get up.*)

SHARAD. No, I am shaking all over. It is a wonder I managed to drive home without an accident. (*He wipes his forehead, which is sweating.*) Now tell me.

SAVITRI. I doubt I know any more than you do. What did she tell you?

SHARAD. When I came back to the office an hour ago, there was a message asking me to call her back. She had called just before ten, Marie said.

SAVITRI. You've had a long day.

SHARAD. Yes, Mrs Pringle's deal has come through, and the way the market is standing still these days, it is cause enough to celebrate, but God (*He wipes himself.*), I called her back and she was as cool as cool can be. Said she had already resigned her job and was going back home. That she wanted to tell me herself so I wouldn't come to know of it secondhand from someone else. And that was all. No reason, nothing. And I couldn't very well ask her any questions, you know how our office cubicles are. Why did she do it? Who is she going with? Do you know him?

SAVITRI. Why do you assume she's going with someone?

SHARAD. Why else would any woman leave her husband and home? And the way you are taking it, I am sure you know a lot more of what is happening but you won't give it away. Please, please tell me. At her age, too, gods help us. She's crazy. (*He looks at Savitri, waiting for her to speak but she says nothing.*)

SHARAD. (*Now hurt more than angry.*) How could she? Without telling us anything at all. Why did I choose this godforsaken eternal winter of a place, except so we could foster a sense of family even though so far from home? Just to be near her so we'd have each other to turn to in time of need. But she never came, never asked for help. (*He is deeply moved.*) She always came to me. Not to Mukund or Hari but always to me. Whether it was to take a sliver from her finger or to help in her arithmetic homework, always she knew she could trust me. Any boy father selected for her, she wanted me to meet him first. Bhau, she'd say, never mind looks, never mind money, make sure, absolutely sure that he won't stand in the way of my studies, she'd say each time. She relied on me and I carried out her trust. And now, (*He holds his head in his hands.*) and now.... (*Angry.*) How could she? Tell me, Savi, you know the story. I'm sure you do. Who is he?

SAVITRI. There is no one else.

SHARAD. Did you ask her?

SAVITRI. There isn't.

SHARAD. So you didn't ask.

SAVITRI. How little you know your sister!

SHARAD. (*Bitterly.*) How little we know anyone. Veejala, my little sister who wouldn't choose her Divali sari without consulting me, leaves her husband and children for some crazy goon.

SAVITRI. Stop jumping to conclusions. There isn't anyone else. She told me.

SHARAD. She did?

SAVITRI. Yes she did, but that is the only thing she told me. She didn't tell me why she was doing what she was doing.

SHARAD. (*Relieved.*) Going home for a holiday is fine. We can always take care of Pixie. (*Worried.*) But why didn't she come down and tell us in person instead of exploding such a bombshell over the phone? And why did she have to resign her job? (*Upset again.*) How could anyone be so imprudent as to give up a job? With all the cutbacks and retrenchments, doesn't she know she can never get it back? She could have taken leave. They'd be only too glad to let her go on loss of salary. I could have advised her, if she had so much as given a hint that she was contemplating something so ridiculous. Did she talk it over with Anant?

SAVITRI. Anant knows.

SHARAD. You are hiding something, Savi.

SAVITRI. I am not *hiding* anything. I just don't see any point in repeating certain things. (*She makes as though to get up but then changes her mind and pours herself another cup of tea. She speaks slowly, deliberately.*) I asked her if she had discussed it with him and she replied that they still spent hours discussing their social schedule—what parties to give and to go to—but that for years they had merely *told* each other their major decisions; they never talked things over.

SHARAD. (*Who has winced at this, speaks hesitantly.*) Are you sure there is no one else, that Anant....

SAVITRI. (*Smiling sympathetically at Sharad's discomfiture.*) Anant? I wonder if we aren't being brainwashed by our environment?—that we can think only of illicit relationships at the root of all troubles. I don't know what Veejala's problem is. We know she does crazy things, but her sense of morality is even more puritanical than mine—the morality she sets up for herself, I mean. I only hope that isn't harming her.

SHARAD. Meaning?

SAVITRI. Never mind. I am content to wait until she is ready to tell me more.

SHARAD. (*Now much calmer.*) Maybe I *will* have some tea. Let me get the newspapers. (*He goes out and returns with the newspapers.*)

SAVITRI. What news of the flood?

SHARAD. Nothing to add to the morning's news. The crest is expected fourth or fifth instead of the seventh. (*He is turning over the pages.*) Oh no! That is why she was in such a rush to tell us!

SAVITRI. What's up?

SHARAD. Oh no! Photograph and all!

SAVITRI. (*Leans over his shoulder and reads aloud parts of the news story, her face showing admiration and delight while Sharad holds his head in his hands and groans.*) " University professor *quits backwoods of Canada for backwoods of India.... Dr Veejala Moghe, assistant professor of astronomy, has resigned her faculty position...claims this is a backwood...where nothing of significance has been done or can be done in her faculty.... Dr Moghe plans to spend the summer at the Pasadena Observatory of the University of California before leaving for her native India.... Asked if conditions were any better in India, she said they were not, but she would feel better wasting her life in her native country than wasting it in the backwoods of Canada. 'This place doesn't exist on any academic map,' she said, 'but my name does, and I'd rather not atrophy here.'...who has published extensively in her field and is a Fellow of the Royal Astronomical Society, was asked why her work had not been recognized at this university. She replied she had never bothered to push herself politically.... Asked if she felt she had been discriminated against because of her sex, Dr Moghe said, 'I happen to be of the wrong colour as well.'"*

SHARAD. Oh God, if she wanted to go, why couldn't she just go quietly instead of drawing us all in? What has she said about Anant and the children?

SAVITRI. Nothing much. Just straight facts. Here, read it.

SHARAD. (*Pushing away the newspaper.*) Not now. My head is splitting.

(*Savitri takes the newpaper off the table and reads the news story again, smiling appreciatively.*)

ACT THREE

Scene I

Lunch hour. Savitri is setting the table for two. Veejala comes in. She is a strikingly good-looking woman in her early forties. Her black hair, waved back, cascades down her shoulders, half-way down her back; she is taller than Savitri, and is wearing an expensive pantsuit and heeled snowboots. Elegant and poised when still, she has masculine confidence when she speaks; the flash of her eyes and the way she blinks deeply are due partly to arrogance and partly to longsightedness. Savitri embraces her warmly. Veejala sits at the table while Savitri fills the soup bowls and plugs in the coffeepot.

VEEJALA. I am sorry to be a little late; the traffic never seems to let up on Fridays.

SAVITRI. Don't worry. I've taken the afternoon off.

VEEJALA. You have! At such short notice? Old man Grierson won't like it.

SAVITRI. He doesn't know. Beverly will manage to get a sub. Anyway, I deserve a break. I haven't called in sick or taken leave in ages, not since Krish cracked his forehead last May and I was called to Emergency.

VEEJALA. You make me feel as though I was dying or something. Taking the day off for my emergency.

SAVITRI. Some people think it is.

VEEJALA. Sharad? Poor bhau, I suppose he's frantic with anxiety.

SAVITRI. He was at first. Now he's moved toward anger, I think.

VEEJALA. I thought he'd be anxious. He always was rather protective about me. I must say I'm disappointed.

SAVITRI. It is hard to worry about you, Vee. You know that all too well. People like to be needed. For some people, the best gift you can give is to ask them for help. But you....

VEEJALA. Yes, it is such an irony that bhau is stuck in this hole. He should be back in Poona, presiding over the family in the mansion—zamindar, dispenser of ancestral wealth, friend of the lessee peasants, godfather to all the village brats who want to get a college education. (*Pushes away the soup that Savitri has placed in front of her.*) No offence, Savi, but I can't down anything. What I need is whiskey, neat, but I don't suppose you'd have it.

SAVITRI. Shall I make you some masala tea?

VEEJALA. You should be there, too. Flapping your shapely bum in a nine-yard sari, Annapurni, generous hostess, brewing masala tea for sore throats and aching hearts.

SAVITRI. If anyone needs to be there, it is you. You could puff away at a cigaret and stomp around in your shorts or bikinis and you'd have gotten the rebel out of your system for a while. Here you have to kill yourself to prove a point, because nothing short of that is rebellion. (*They look at each other across the table*.)

VEEJALA. Why are we being so crabby to each other?

SAVITRI. (*Swallowing the tears in her eyes and smiling*.) Because.

VEEJALA. (*Leaning forward intensely*.) Don't you know why I did it? Don't you understand?

SAVITRI. No.

VEEJALA. I'd hoped you would, at least you.

SAVITRI. There are many things about you I don't understand, Vee, but that has never come between us.

VEEJALA. (*Quietly*.) And this has?

SAVITRI. (*Quietly*.) No, it hasn't. Perhaps it should, but it hasn't.

VEEJALA. But you don't approve.

SAVITRI. I don't know. I've always held that when an essentially moral person does something usually considered immoral, it is more likely to have moral reasons than immoral.

VEEJALA. But in this, you don't?

SAVITRI. I don't know, Vee, I don't know. What can I say except the usual things. That at least for the children's sake....

VEEJALA. The children don't need me. A child grows as a flower grows.

SAVITRI. But it grows better when there is sunshine and there aren't weeds. (*Shakes her head*.) No, it is so hard not to fall into clichés.

VEEJALA. Because this is a cliché situation? A woman walking out on her husband? (*Savitri shakes her head*.) Okay, okay. (*Veejala leans her elbow on the table and presses her forehead and speaks slowly*.) The children. They are not really ours. They are their own, and all too soon they realize that. When Vithal went off that summer, I missed him, oh, how I missed him, and yet when he came back, everything was changed. He was his own world, set in his ways, self-contained, the umbilical cord broken off. Everything seemed the same, but it wasn't. I wonder if that's how our mothers felt when we got married. I remember my first visit at rakhi time the autumn I got married. Oh, I was so happy to be back, it was like rolling back into the niche where I belonged. And yet, maybe it wasn't so to mother. Come to think of it, I was pampered and indulged in, an honoured guest. That's probably how mother felt about me, just as I felt about Vithal. A pain, an excruciating pain where the cord had been pulled off, deep, deep in the guts, but something final. No, it is not the children I will miss or worry about.... I have always been something of a magpie. It is Anant. Already I feel as though I've left half my self behind.... But it is a half that is best left behind. (*Silence for a moment.*)

SAVITRI. It is the suddenness of it all. Even I didn't know it was coming. One could see the problems, of course, the incompatibilities, that others wouldn't have. But then every marriage, every job has some of that. And we haven't had more than the usual share. So why?

VEEJALA. That's not it, that's not it at all. I don't know, Savi. It is my turn to say that.

SAVITRI. Maybe you are still just a spoiled brat.

VEEJALA. Maybe. Or maybe it is my last desperate attempt to do something worthwhile. Instead of being tied down to a bloodless rat race. Twenty-five thousand a year and no sweat to speak of. A handsome scientist for a husband and two lovely children. An eighty-thousand-dollar house and the whole works. Everything one could ever wish for. And yet when I look through that telescope and see the stars, when I watch the shimmering dance of Borealis, I feel I have to go have one last crack at real scholarship. Leave everything and follow me, he said, and right away Simon, who was called Peter, left everything and followed him.

(*Phone rings. Savitri picks it up.*)

SAVITRI. I am feeling better, thanks, Bev. Any problems? Yes, Mr Grierson.... Did you try Cindy? She's usually home at lunch time.... Well, they are working on their project for the first hour and.... I suppose I could come out for the last two classes.... No, I am sorry there is no way I can get myself out for the first hour.... Yes I'll be there. (*Hangs up.*)

VEEJALA. Sucker, every time a sucker, Savi. I know. I heard. You have to go. You are so unrelentingly sweet.

SAVITRI. (*Smiling.*) So unrelentingly stupid, that is all. I think everyone should be taught how to tell a lie. It is as essential as knowing how to fall the right way in hockey or football. But you take your time, Vee, rest for a while.

VEEJALA. Don't worry about me. Get back to your sheep.

(*Savitri hastily finishes her lunch and starts clearing away the table.*)

VEEJALA. (*To herself more than to Savitri.*) I am not young. I can't concentrate even an hour on anything I read. My eyes are half gone. And I haven't churned out even my usual quota of papers these two years...throwing away a pearl of great price for something glowing in the dark that could well be a leopard's eyes staring at the kill.

Scene II

Same scene as before. Veejala is at the table, coffee mug and several magazines in front of her. She has her legs up on the chair across. Sunlight streams in from the left. Jyoti is taking off her boots.

JYOTI. (*Guardedly.*) Hullo, auntie.

VEEJALA. Hullo, Jyu!

JYOTI. Been here long? Had lunch?

VEEJALA. Yes, thanks, you?

JYOTI. Sort of. Mom home?

VEEJALA. No, she was here but now she's back at work. I should be going too. Have a 3:40 class. (*Jyoti helps herself to a pop from the refrigerator.*)

VEEJALA. How are things? How's Andre?

JYOTI. (*Distantly.*) He's alright, thanks.

VEEJALA. None of my business, in other words.

JYOTI. (*Her back turned to Veejala as she opens a cabinet for a glass.*) It *is* your business, auntie, just as it is mine to ask you what is happening. But we've lost the ability to ask and answer.

VEEJALA. (*After a moment's silence.*) We are lucky as long as we can have one or two to whom we can still talk.

JYOTI. If. But everything burns up one's hand. You feel real close to someone and then bang slam, the door shuts on your face. (*Jyoti turns as if to go away, but then sits at the table, back to the sun.*) Sridhar, I thought I could really talk to him.

VEEJALA. We are all pretty dumb at times, Jyu, but surely you are not so dumb that you didn't know he was head over heels in love with you?

JYOTI. I could talk to him, I really could.

VEEJALA. One can never talk to the ones closest to oneself.

JYOTI. I didn't know he was that close to me. I guess I was misled by his insistence that I was. Anyway, it is all far too confusing right now. Let's talk about you. (*She is more relaxed.*)

VEEJALA. What makes you think that's any less confusing?

JYOTI. You've taken action. One can't come to that without having resolved the confusion.

VEEJALA. It could be that one takes action thinking one has resolved it. But then one might find oneself still confused. Hasn't that happened to you? After you first made love, for instance?

JYOTI. (*Angrily.*) Mom has—

VEEJALA. Certainly not. Savi hasn't told me anything.

JYOTI. (*Sarcastically.*) Just a shot in the dark.

VEEJALA. And you were dumb enough to give yourself away.

JYOTI. It shows in my eyes, eh? The sparkle of stars and all that.

VEEJALA. More in one's hips after a while, I believe. Mine was a shot in the dark. But those aunts and great aunts back home, they developed some kind of sixth sense, maybe. I wish I had picked up some of the tidbits of knowledge teenagers pick up just listening to those women. (*She goes on reminiscently.*) They didn't miss anything, I can tell you, even though they seldom left the house compound. I remember how Kamal...well, I won't bore you with old tales. Sign of old age. Must guard myself against that, eh! Frankly, I simply assumed you were no virgin. It is the tight-lipped type that gives in, the so-called loose ones who let themselves be patted and stroked by one and all hang on to their virginity a lot longer. (*Jyoti is close to tears. Veejala notices it, gets up impulsively, and embraces her.*)

VEEJALA. That was mean of me, Jyu, I am sorry. And ashamed. Treating you like a grown-up. I am on your side, Jyoti; it is a beautiful experience, quite quite ravishing, shall we say? (*She kisses Jyoti on the forehead and strokes her hair.*) It will be very confusing for a while even without the gossip. And gossip will be hard to take. Everyone will say you are a fool to choose a long-haired, hip-type foreigner when you have a clean-cut intelligent Hindu waiting on you. But tell them that if this were India, their counterparts would be saying the same thing about Sridhar the alien southerner; oh, oh, there I go again, assumed like an old fogie that you were planning to marry one of them. You don't have to, Jyoti. Sharad would kill me if he heard me give you this advice, but it is as sound a piece of advice for anyone living today in this country—jump into bed as many times as you wish, but don't jump into matrimony. We, born and brought up in another age and another culture, know that marriage is for keeps, and we are willing to make a million adjustments, but you kids who grow up here are so rigid in your expectations, so lax in your commitment, you throw in the towel the minute something goes wrong. Your uncle and I would have been divorced a dozen times if we hadn't the background we have. Both of us have been outrageously irresponsible; I've done the craziest things when we had money, and you know about most of them; and he's been the reason we never had much money for the first million years we were students. Why do you think it took me ten years to get my degree? I was working at odd jobs— library, dishwashing, waitressing, in addition to my assistantship—anything I could get....

JYOTI. You were? You mean you were poor?

VEEJALA. As a churchmouse.

JYOTI. But why?

VEEJALA. Ah, there were reasons, my love. Those were great times, Jyoti. Such experiences as few can have. We were both A-plus students. And crazy. One has to be a little crazy if one is to do anything worthwhile. My first paper, back in '61, was quite something. Pasadena, that's why I am going there, Pasadena was my starting point. I was shaking like a leaf the whole time I was presenting the paper, and a very pregnant leaf, too. I wanted to go back to my room and sleep, but then there were questions and discussions on the paper that went on longer than I've ever seen. As soon as I could get away I ran to our room and threw up. That was some scene. Vithal, open mouthed and ready to bawl, Anant frantic, and who should knock? Professor Steiner, come to congratulate me. Steiner in person, and me doubled up over the washbasin. '61, wonderful, sad '61.

JYOTI. You lost the baby right then?

VEEJALA. No, two weeks later, back home, thank God. You needn't look so commiserating, Jyu, I couldn't have cared less at the time. Success was so heady, so absobloominutely great, it was a fair bargain—recognition in exchange for a five-month-old fetus. I got seventy-three requests for copies of my paper that first year. A fair and square bargain dealt out by fate. You have to pay a price for everything and I've never regretted that. But now, what am I getting for the high price of inertia that I am paying? There was no answer to that. Which is why I am striking out.

JYOTI. Pasadena, London, Delhi, it sounds exciting and wonderful. And (*Hesitantly.*) so reassuring to know that you are not breaking up with Uncle Anant for...just for the breaking up.

VEEJALA. You would like to be really sure of that, wouldn't you? (*Jyoti nods, half eager, half afraid. Veejala draws her head to her breast.*) We are all in one godamnawful mess, my love, but still lucky; we have one or two we can hold on to.

And now I am going to rest for a few minutes in Savi's ever ready guest room. (*Exits.*)

(*Lights dim and immediately go up on the same scene. There is no one in the kitchen, but Jyoti and Andre are talking offstage on the back landing. Their shadows dance on the kitchen wall.*)

JYOTI. (*Her voice is still calm but a little louder than usual.*) Not this week, Andre, please don't pester me.

ANDRE. (*Loud and angry.*) Pester you! I've been away almost a week, and you refuse me a date.

JYOTI. Oh, Andre, please don't ask me. I missed you, missed you so much. If only you didn't have to go, if you hadn't gone, maybe....

ANDRE. Maybe what? Come on, honey bun, just a couple of hours.

JYOTI. (*With quiet firmness.*) No, Andre, no. I could give you half a dozen reasons. I am working all week evenings, I have two final exams coming up, mom's car has to go to the garage, all true, but they aren't *the* reason. It is me. I am confused. I have to sort things out.

ANDRE. What things? You said the same thing over the phone. What d'you mean. I have a car, love.

JYOTI. Things, you and me. I need time.

ANDRE. Damn it, how can you be so cool, so rational. One day I'll get into your inner kernel of stillness. I swear I will tear my way into that silence and hear you scream of lust and pain. God, you stand there as though nothing moves you, but I know, goddamnit, I know you are a cauldron of emotions sealed four times over. (*Sound of back door slamming. Jyoti comes in and takes her place at the window. Veejala comes in.*)

JYOTI. I didn't think you could have heard.

VEEJALA. Not hear a tornado? What in you brings out such violence, Jyoti? I grant you are not quite the average kid next door, but this, oof.

JYOTI. What do you think I should be feeling?

VEEJALA. Hm. I think you should be thrilled to pieces, to use Pixie's phrase, to have aroused such a passion in someone.

JYOTI. I am nothing. Just a blank wall or mirror or something. Each one sees himself in me. I have nothing to do with anything they feel. I am just nothing in myself. Maybe that's why I arouse violence.... And yet, the other day I felt so warm and today I feel so distant.

VEEJALA. We are far too serious about everything. Why don't we just laugh, roll around in the snow, build a snowcastle.

JYOTI. (*Intensely*.) May I come with you to India? I've always wanted to travel around India. It seems so far away, so blurred, even though I was eleven or twelve when we left. Please.

VEEJALA. (*Lightly*.) I'd have said yes right away if I hadn't heard the cyclone shooting through. To tell you the truth, Jyoti, I *have* regretted that miscarriage. It was a girl. I've burned with envy a million times, love, seeing you and Savitri together. And the only reason I haven't wooed you closer to myself is because I know how much I want you there. So maybe I'd have refused to take you even sans cyclone.

JYOTI. Say that again. I lost you.

VEEJALA. Never mind. Now that I heard all this thunder, I have to say that you have to face up to your problems, you can't run away from them, not with me nowise. I'll let you in on another secret, Jyoti; for several years I've wanted to quit and strike out as I'm doing now, but things weren't quite right between Anant and myself. And if I'd left then, I might have felt guilty all the time that I was running away from something that I perhaps did not want rather than going toward something I want with all my soul. But now all is fine between us.

JYOTI. Do you really have to go? Vithal needs you.

VEEJALA. Anyone else would have said Priti needs me. But you know me better.

JYOTI. Vithal is only an excuse. I need you. Please.

VEEJALA. We are all in one godawful mess, my darling, but we'll survive.

Scene III

Basement. Savitri is ironing, Jyoti is folding Savitri's colourful saris.

SAVITRI. Don't think I haven't recognized your contempt for us who have been faithful all our lives, Jyoti. It hurts, but I know that too is a form of idealism—to think that love is free, not to be bound.... And I believe love is free....

Love makes one beautiful, so so breathtakingly beautiful. Your cousin Kanta, I remember when her mother was in love. That was my first experience of love, it was at second hand, of course, as first experiences often are. She was staying with us that year, going to college. It was one of my best years because when someone is in love she can give and receive affection so purely, so spontaneously, that the happiness keeps spreading in concentric circles, drawing more and more people into itself. Oh, she was beautiful....

JYOTI. What happened then?

SAVITRI. What happens to so many girls. There was a big hullaballoo and she was married off to a rich widower who lived so far away he couldn't have heard any of this gossip. She's spent her life milking cows and supervising the measuring of the harvest. But (*Her eyes shine with remembrance.*) she had *it*, Jyoti, for only a few months, but she had the real thing. That is why I feel so much for you, for your sadness.

JYOTI. (*Softly.*) It is not the real thing, is that what it means?

SAVITRI. (*After a pause.*) If I were sure of that, I would tell you so.

JYOTI. I don't want to believe it, mom, first love, it is my first love. (*Her voice breaks.*)

(*Savitri pauses in her ironing and looks at her. But Jyoti has already recovered.*)

JYOTI. (*In normal voice.*) I think you've missed this part. It needs to be redone.

SAVITRI. (*Taking the sari from her, she says half seriously, half jokingly.*) Never consummate your first love, and you'll have it all your life—Mother Philomena used to say it at the end-of-the-year counselling to us.

JYOTI. (*Casually.*) Did you have one, mom?

SAVITRI. (*Laughing.*) Now, now, Jyoti, how am I supposed to answer that? If I say I didn't, I'd plummet down in your esteem! (*Points her thumb downward.*)

JYOTI. And if you said you did?

SAVITRI. Probably I would plummet down sometime later.

JYOTI. We need to know, mom, we've got to know more about our parents. We never do. I've sometimes wondered, mom, wondered in what senseless moment of upward kicking of legs and flailing arms I was conceived.

SAVITRI. (*Matter-of-factly.*) Would it help if I said you were conceived in the springtime of my love, in the floodtide of desire? It is true, but would it really help? As for knowing about one's parents, we don't need facts. My parents were so different, now that I see their personalities from my experience I see so much more, but when I was a child, a girl, even a young woman, I naturally and blindly believed my parents were an open book to one another, that there was no secret anywhere.

JYOTI. But that's how I see you and dad!

SAVITRI. All is not lost, my munchkin. One day may you be as happy as I have been.

Scene IV

Phone rings. Jyoti enters from the back door at the fourth ring. She has just come in from the outside—she has on her winter coat and boots. In the ensuing scene, Jyoti speaks into the kitchen phone while on the other side of the stage Sridhar is speaking from a telephone booth.

JYOTI. Hullo.

SRIDHAR. Hullo, Jyoti.

JYOTI. Hi, Shri. Wait a sec while I take off my coat. I've just come in.

SRIDHAR. I know. I saw you.

JYOTI. Saw me? Where?

SRIDHAR. As you turned off King's Drive.

JYOTI. And you didn't bother to give me a ride. Boy, some folks can be mean.

SRIDHAR. Would you have accepted?

JYOTI. (*Evading the question.*) What were you doing there at this time of day?

SRIDHAR. Following you.

(*Jyoti's colour rises. She opens her mouth as though to say something, but her lips tremble and she says nothing.*)

SRIDHAR. (*His voice less strained now.*) You didn't think all those "chance encounters" over the last year were accidental, did you? I made an ass of myself the other day. I've been slapping myself ever since. So suicidal of me, to blast the ground from under my feet. I suppose that's the end? (*The last question is in a very low, strained voice.*)

(*Jyoti doesn't reply.*)

SRIDHAR. I've been going over those few minutes ever since. When I started spouting my great rhetoric, there was a moment when I could have stopped myself. But I went on, quite sure it would do me good to get it out of my system. God, what an ass. (*Jyoti does not reply but there are tears gathering in her eyes.*) We can't meet on the same footing any more...can we?

JYOTI. No.

SRIDHAR. Quoth the raven, Nevermore. (*He tries to sound flippant.*)

JYOTI. (*Slowly.*) Not on that footing but maybe, maybe on....

SRIDHAR. (*Incredulous and overjoyed.*) Jyoti! (*More his usual self.*) You mean you haven't thrown me out on my ear? That we can, we might, with a bit of amnesia, talk again? May I come over now?

JYOTI. (*Her eyes clearer now.*) Hey, hey, not so fast.

(*She disconnects the call with her free hand and stands cradling the receiver, running her fingers over the mouthpiece as lights dim.*)

Scene V

Jayant is having a Coke at the kitchen table. The phone rings.

JAYANT. (*Picking up the receiver.*) Hullo.

PRITI. (*At the other end.*) Jai? Oh, Jaida, thank God you are home. (*Panic and relief come through clearly in her voice as she speaks.*)

JAYANT. (*With concern and tenderness on his face but in a normal, special voice.*) Hi! Pixie Trix! Whassa matta? Boogeyman a-chasing you? Wanna Big Brave to rescue you?

PRITI. Oh Jai, can you pick us up? We are stranded.

JAYANT. Where? What do you mean "we"? Who?

PRITI. At Polo Park, Laura and me. Mommy was to pick us up at 5:30 but she hasn't come.

JAYANT. (*Under his breath.*) Jeesus. It is 6:20!

PRITI. And she hasn't come yet. And the stores are all closed and the people all gone.

JAYANT. (*To himself angrily.*) God, how irresponsible can one get? She doesn't deserve to have kids. (*To Priti soothingly.*) Chin up, bebe. Where are you now?

PRITI. Near Eaton's. Just where mommy told us to be.

JAYANT. Walk back through the mall to the door near Sears.

PRITI. But mommy told us to wait here. Why hasn't she come. (*In tears.*) She said she would.

JAYANT. You know how mommy has a hundred and thirty-nine things on her mind twenty-eight hours a day, Pixie. Both of you go to the Sears door—the Bread and Key entrance, get it? Near the cinema. And stay between the doors. And don't worry. People will

140 *The Door I Shut Behind Me*

soon be coming to the movie. And store managers will soon be coming out, too, from every store. And there will be people at the bus stop, get it? And listen, even if your mum does turn up, don't take off. Stay on until I come down. Clear? Go straight to the cinema place and stay put. I'll be there in twenty minutes. Got a watch?

PRITI. Laura has hers.

JAYANT. Good, remember I can't reach you till twenty minutes from now. Take a look at the watch now, else you'll think it is an hour after five minutes.

PRITI. Okay, shall I hang up?

JAYANT. K.O. Pixie-Trix. (*Hangs up, checks that he has his car keys in his pocket, and rushes out without a coat.*)

Scene VI

An hour later. Jayant comes in, followed by Priti and Laura, whose chattering voices precede them. Priti runs through the kitchen and comes back with a volume of Brittanica.

PRITI. Here. There's twenty pages of stuff on Egypt here. Enough for two projects.

JAYANT. Sit down, Laura, I am going to make some hot chocolate for all of us.

LAURA. No thanks, I am late for dinner as is. Thanks for the ride, Jai. And bye, Priti. (*Pronouncing it "Pretty."*) I'll return this tomorrow.

PRITI. I don't need that volume for my project. Keep it as long as you want to. (*Laura leaves. Jayant warms milk in a saucepan and takes out a can of Quik. Priti sits at the table; suddenly she bursts out crying, head buried in her arms.*)

PRITI. (*Sobbing.*) What am I going to do? What am I gonna do?

JAYANT. What's eating ma petite princess?

PRITI. Three times this week I was late to school. And today she forgot altogether.

JAYANT. Just a rough patch, munchkin. You know all about life under a volcano. A rumble here, a tremor there. But you should be used to it by now. Come on, take it easy.

PRITI. Three days. You don't know Miss Grindley. Takes a ratch even for no reason. And you know the school rules. Three times late and you are finished. You don't know our school.

JAYANT. I thought you liked this school. Your mum was praising it so much. Said you enjoyed it.

PRITI. Now I know why she put me there. Cos we have a residence. That's why. So she can leave me and not have to worry about me when there is no home left.

JAYANT. (*Angrily.*) Bull (*He pauses.*) —y for you. (*Tenderly.*) What's this if not your home, you silly goose. Next year you shall stay right here. And meanwhile I shall drive you to school every morning.

PRITI. (*Taking it as a game.*) Promise by the hair on your chinny chinny chin?

JAYANT. Promise by the hair on my chinny chinny chin.

PRITI. Cross your heart and hope to die?

JAYANT. Cross my heart and hope to die.

PRITI. (*Totally relaxed.*) Sounds good, Jai. Only one teeny weeny snag. You're leaving.

JAYANT. Can't. I've promised to be your chauffeur.

PRITI. (*Handing him an imaginary paper.*) Here, take back your promise. I don't want to stop you from making your fortune in your seven league boots.

JAYANT. Can't. A promise is a promise is a kick in the butt if I break it.

PRITI. You shouldn't upset all your plans for a silly little problem like mine. I can take the bus. Even if I do have to get up at 6:30 to get to that stupid bus that always leaves just as ours reaches the corner. But (*Plaintively.*) I wish mommy wouldn't say she'd take me; then I get up late and she gets up late anyway and by the time we leave...she thinks it is okay to be a few minutes late, but it isn't. We just have to be in by 8:45. We just have to. (*She is close to tears again.*)

JAYANT. Eight o'clock every morning now to the end of June. I'll pick you up on the dot of eight, and if you aren't ready, oh boy, you'll get it from me, forget Miss Grouchy.

PRITI. (*Laughing.*) Grindley.

JAYANT. Whatever. But keep it a secret for now. I'll come Monday morning and we'll spill it then, okay?

PRITI. But you are all set to go!

JAYANT. I'll stay. If there's a Christly chance for me to do something for someone, I'd gladly stay put. Jeesus, how dispensable we are. I'd stay even if that stupid parakeet of yours said it needed me to clean its cage. How much more readily for you.... Here, a glutton aren't you? Didn't leave a drop for me. (*Takes up the saucepan and turns it upside down.*)

Scene VII

Sunday, shortly after noon, through the glass of the patio doors in the living room can be seen a five-foot evergreen tree with snow packed all around its base. While the snow against the garage wall in the background is two feet high, the rest of the yard has been walked on or shovelled almost to the grass. Vithal and Jayant are standing near the patio door looking out, beer cans in hand. Sridhar is stretched on a couch.

JAYANT. (*Looking at his right palm.*) Jeesus, am I ever in for blisters! Right through the work gloves and all!

VITHAL. Growing soft, are we?

JAYANT. That tree weighs half a ton. And prickly as a porcupine too.

SRIDHAR. Man, what d'you expect if not blisters? You were shovelling like a demon was in you. Now, can you tell me all about this farewell present? I just drop by, for a minute, and next thing I know I am shovelling and snorting in the snow.

JAYANT. No farewells. I ain't going.

SRIDHAR. You crazy or something, man?

VITHAL. Or maybe sane for once. Our brother here has decided to go sandbagging instead, along St Mary's, or maybe St Norbert. Service before self. Tamasoma Jyotir Gamaya—from darkness lead me to light.

JAYANT. Cut it out, Vith. I am dropping out of the trip because Jim's girlfriend has joined the gang, and who wants to be saddled up with a girl, Jeesus, no way.

VITHAL. Pixie said something about you being her chauffeur.

JAYANT. That kid is a blabbermouth. I dunno what she's talking about. D'you think the ice would hold a coupla weeks? We sure packed that snow in. Should be like concrete for at least a while.

VITHAL. If the temp goes up to zero degrees midweek, as they expect, that would be the end of that. (*He waves at the tree.*)

JAYANT. So what? (*Vehemently.*) What does it matter how long it stands? The point is that it *is* there, beautiful and green for the length of its life. A day, a hundred thousand days, it is a question of what we do and are, during that time. This evergreen doesn't have one Christly use—it isn't even good as firewood—but it is there and it is green, it is beautiful.

SRIDHAR. And rootless.

JAYANT. Yeah, rootless. Let's face it, Jeesus, no one, but no one has roots anywhere because that's the way things are in 1979 A.D.

But we can stand tall, man, and live each day for all it's godamned worth and ours. And now I'm going for a shower. Never thought one could sweat oneself to stink just shovelling snow.

(*Doorbell rings. Jayant goes to the door and opens it. Veejala enters. Sridhar springs up as Jayant helps her out of her coat.*)

VEEJALA. Have the pizzas been delivered? I'm sorry I'm late.

(*Priti, Krish, Jyoti, and Anant have come in behind Veejala, carrying cartons of soft drinks and potato and taco chips.*)

VEEJALA. (*Coming in.*) Hullo Sridhar! Vithal, this is a wonderful surprise. We were so hoping you'd come home for dinner last night. I had borrowed Jyoti and Krish, seeing as I never get to have my own children with me. (*She embraces him.*) Sweetheart, have you been on a construction site? There's sawdust or something in your hair, and you've been perspiring. (*She runs her hand through his hair and embraces him again.*) Well, I got late picking up the kids from the skating rink, and so I ordered pizza delivered here. I knew Savi and Sharad would have gone to the temple today. They should be back any minute, and we are going to be one big happy family for one last time, until you come back, Jai.

VITHAL. News, news, Jayant is staying back.

JAYANT. Because Jim's girlfriend insists on coming and—

SRIDHAR. Who wants to be saddled with a girl?

Uma Parameswaran

THE PERFORATED SHEET
Essays on Salman Rushdie's Art

Much has been said about Salman Rushdie's art. The different ways in which he moulds reams of material, endless and disjointed, into delightfully intricate and refreshingly original patterns.

Uma Parameswaran certainly does him credit. Her lively essays, the first major study of Rushdie's fiction, introduce one to the subtleties and nuances of his singing prose. Simplistic in their approach, these self-contained essays dwell on the various aspects of his writing, providing much pleasure and information.

Far from being a heavy literary tome, this eminently readable collection can be enjoyed by both scholars and ordinary readers alike.